A PLACE IN HISTORY

Paul Johnson was born in 1928 and
educated at Stonyhurst and Magdalen
College, Oxford, where he read history. He
worked in Paris as Deputy Editor
of the international edition of the French
magazine *Réalités* and was also Paris
Correspondent of the *New Statesman*. In 1955
he became Assistant Editor of the
New Statesman, later Deputy Editor and
(1965–70) Editor. His lifelong interest
has been the study of history and he
is the author of 'The Offshore Islanders',
'The Life and Times of Edward III' and
'Elizabeth I: A Study in Power and
Intellect'. Paul Johnson is now a full-time
historian and political commentator
and is engaged at present on a one-volume
'History of Christianity'.

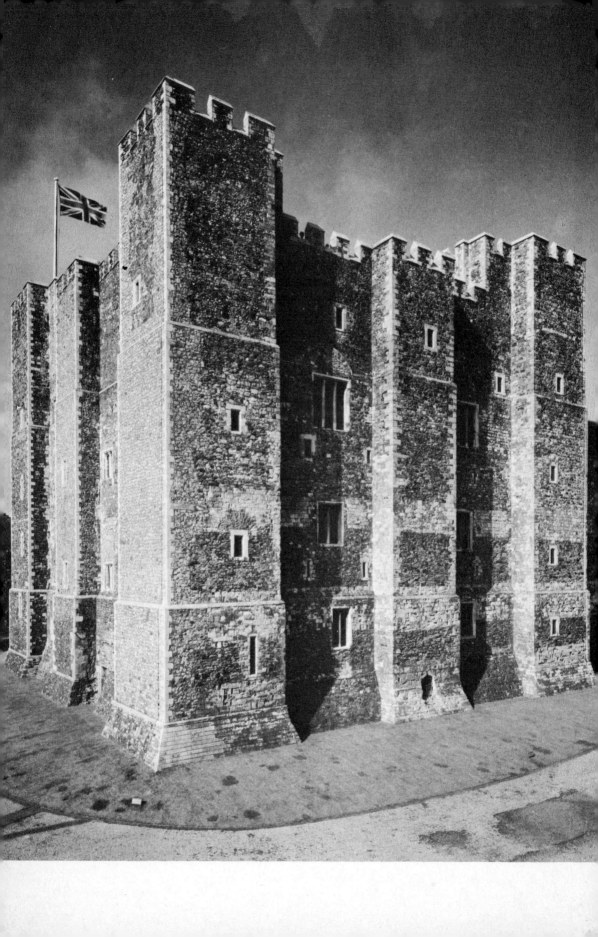

A PLACE IN HISTORY

PAUL JOHNSON

Weidenfeld & Nicolson

Frontispiece Dover Castle – Keep

First published in Great Britain in May 1974 by
George Weidenfeld and Nicolson Ltd
Second impression October 1974

ISBN 0 297 76757 7

Filmset and printed Offset Litho in
Great Britain by Cox and Wyman Ltd,
London, Fakenham and Reading

CONTENTS

PREFACE

This little book of essays is designed to accompany, in written and pictorial form, a series of documentary films presented by Thames Television. Although the choice of subjects was determined by Thames TV, any assertions made or conclusions reached in the essays are, of course, my own. Their object is not unduly ambitious. They do not collectively attempt to present a general view of British history. My aim has been to show how and why certain places, at specific periods, have made an important contribution to the evolution of British society and its institutions. In some cases, the place selected has had a bearing on our affairs for many centuries, and continues to influence them even today; in others, it has emerged briefly into the spotlight of history and then retreated into its shadows. Thus, St David's in Pembrokeshire was the centre of an emergent Celtic-Christian culture, during the early Dark Ages, and was in time by-passed by stronger historical forces. In some respects, the society which made St David's possible still existed at Glencoe at the end of the seventeenth century, when a tragic and bloody episode epitomized the irresistible pressures which were destroying the last remnants of tribalism in Britain. The doom of the Glencoe MacDonalds, one might say, had already been adumbrated, more than a century before, by the triumph of the Scottish Reformation in St Andrews, which ensured that the Scottish lowlands would be increasingly linked to the dominant patterns of the South, and thus become a springboard for the penetration of the Highlands. And in turn, events in the Scottish Lowlands were influenced by the development in London's Whitehall of a strong central administration, directing the resources of the paramount power in Britain.

One theme in these essays, therefore, is the significant connections which can be established between different places and their historical roles. But another theme is continuity: the way in which certain places have touched national life over vast periods of time. Berkeley Castle illustrates the tenacity, the sheer power of survival, of a great landed and political family operating for nearly a millennium from the fortress it built and embellished.

7

For an even longer period, Norwich and its neighbourhood have demonstrated the vitality of English provincial society and its multifarious contributions to our culture and politics. Sometimes the function of a place changes, as the British genius for improvisation finds new uses for its buildings and geographical virtues: no better example can be found than Whitehall itself, an archiepiscopal palace which became a royal court and then the habitat of government. Greenwich transformed itself from a royal palace into a centre of naval administration and welfare, and astronomy. It is now both a naval museum and a college of higher naval studies, including thermonuclear warfare. Past, present and future, as it were, lie in an incongruous but placid juxtaposition. The legal sanctum of the Inner and Middle Temple was once the English headquarters of ecclesiastical banker-knights. Since then it has promoted the development of English jurisprudence from within an ancient fabric which has been constantly renewed and rebuilt, but which still contains the venerable church as its focus. St Bartholomew's Hospital evolved from a religious alms-house: its continuous existence over eight centuries reflects both the history of medical science and the changing attitudes of society towards the needs of the unfortunate. Ironbridge in Shropshire witnessed the slow gestation over many centuries, and then the rapid and dramatic birth, of a new industrial civilization, which, in a few generations, left the area – in the true sense of the word – effete, its historic task accomplished. The Royal Institution was founded to propagate and popularise the new scientific and technical skills which the age of Ironbridge had placed at the disposal of mankind. Brighton, in turn, came into vibrant existence to exploit the new demands for health and leisure – initially for the élite, increasingly for the many – which industrial wealth and technology made possible. And beyond Brighton was, and is, the English Channel, the salient determining geographical factor which, sometimes visibly, often imperceptibly, has influenced Britain's growth as a separate island-state and thus impinged on all the places and institutions described above.

One cannot walk far in Britain without treading on the past; or, indeed, catching glimpses of its visible shape, in brick and slate, in stone and painted glass, in wrought or cast-iron, in carved oak and sculptured marble. This book attempts to show how thirteen different localities have earned their place in our history, and how the interplay of a building or a site, with the men and women who have lived there, the ideas they held, the institutions they served, has determined the course of events, and so helped to produce the world we inhabit in the 1970s. It will have served its modest purpose of it encourages the reader to visit or re-visit these places, and if it illuminates what he or she finds there.

Iver, Buckinghamshire   Paul Johnson
October 1973

St David's Cathedral, with
the remains of the Bishop's
Palace in the foreground.

1 ST DAVID'S CATHEDRAL

The World of Celtic Christianity

ST DAVID'S, on the rocky tip of the Pembrokeshire peninsula, does not strike the modern visitor – to put it mildly – as an obvious site for a cathedral. It is, to be sure, a place of great beauty. The ancient church itself, despite its harsh restoration by Gilbert Scott in the 1860s, seems as though it were enfolded in the land, almost part of it. The dull, purplish sandstone of which it is built is best seen on a moonlit night, when it is possible to entertain the fancy that it grew naturally from the rocky soil, like the daffodils which surround it in spring. Nor is this effect accidental, for the building is irregular, following the uneven contours of the ground, and it was placed in the hollow deliberately, to conceal its size and wealth from sea-raiders nosing their war galleys around the coast. From the gate, thirty-nine steps drop down to the door of the cathedral; and, inside it, the floor slopes upwards three feet to the altar. As an architectural composition, its forms and colours thus blend perfectly with the landscape. But why place a cathedral here at all? St David's is remote and hard of access even today. The roads, such as they are, are narrow, the population sparse, the cliffs monumental, the sea often savage. Gales of sixty to eighty miles an hour are not only frequent, but normal at certain seasons; and on 29 November 1954, the anemometer at Brawdy Naval Air Station, near St David's, registered its limit – 130 mph. This is a harsh and poor district; St Patrick, who probably first built a chapel on the site, referred to it as *in ultimis terrae*, 'at the ends of the earth'. What possessed the founders of St David's to think it suitable as the headquarters of their mission?

Yet to ask this question is to betray a misunderstanding of the Celtic church, of the geography which shaped it, and of its purpose and culture. The Celtic world, in both its pre-Christian and post-Christian manifestations, was internationalist, maritime and rural. It spread, indeed, westward from central Europe; but it is more correct to describe the Celts as cultural harbingers and transmitters, rather than a race. They did not conquer in millions, like a gigantic wave, submerging other races beneath them; they penetrated in thousands, bringing with them a language, an economy, an aesthetic and a complex of attitudes to life and nature. They proselytized, and the peoples they suborned accepted their culture, which was patriarchal, pastoral, introspective and other-worldly. By contrast, the civilization of Rome was logical like their language, legalistic and hierarchical like their institutions, highly disciplined and methodical, like their armies; above all, urban. In Celtic Gaul, the Roman conquest and penetration was complete, except in Brittany – a western peninsula so similar in its structure and ecology to Cornwall and Pembrokeshire. In the rest of what we now call France, the Latin or Romance culture established itself so firmly that it was later able to envelop and absorb the Germanic-speaking Franks who poured in from the north-east. But in the British Isles the Roman conquest was incomplete. Even in the settled areas of Britain, east of the Welsh Marches, south of the Roman wall, the cultural impress of Rome was superficial. Their cities did not, on the whole, flourish as on the Continent. The small, Romanized upper class spoke Latin, apparently in a very pure form; the bulk of the population knew nothing but pidgin, for their tongue remained Celtic. Moreover, the most ambitious of Roman governors, Agricola, was never allowed to complete his conquest of Scotland, or to set foot in Ireland (though he glimpsed it from across the sea); and Wales, except in the far south-east, was held as a frontier-colony, exploited for its minerals but not settled according to Roman norms.

The failure, or partial failure, of the Roman experiment in the British Isles was inevitably reflected in its ecclesiastical structures when the civil and military authority of Rome retired and Christianity became, as it were, the residual legatee of the empire. The extent of Christian penetration of Britain during the Roman period is conjectural; but from the early fourth century it was, of course, the official religion of the empire. Part of the population was Christianized, churches were built – one, perhaps, at Glastonbury in Somerset, always reputed to have been the first Christian foundation in the country. Certainly, when Augustine and his mission came to Kent, in the late sixth century, they were able to build their first church on the site of an ancient chapel. But the invasions of Jutes, Angles and Saxons tended to push Christianity westwards, into the areas where Celtic culture was still dominant, and where the Romans had scarcely penetrated, if at all.

Thus, in the early Dark Ages, we see emerging in the British Isles two varieties of Christianity: one, sponsored by Rome, as part of a deliberate missionary work, spreading its way up the East Coast in the seventh and eighth centuries and penetrating inland; the other, Celtic in culture, much earlier in origin, gradually replacing pagan forms in the west. This Celtic Christianity had as its geographical centre not the land, but the waters of the Irish Sea. Its communications were essentially maritime, between Ireland and Scotland, between Ireland and Wales, and indeed with Rome itself. What we know about this

A Celtic Cross in the churchyard at Nevern. Celtic Christianity had as its geographical centre not the land, but the waters of the Irish Sea.

early Celtic church is meagre, at any rate in written sources, and all of these are copies, or compilations, or even pious inventions dating from much later periods. Moreover, in this age, clerics did not write accounts of events for the benefit of future historians but to impress the faithful: their writings were homilies, not records. All the same, we can be reasonably sure that St Patrick played a dominant part in the creation of this Celtic Christian confederation, and the probability is that he came from the part of Wales where St David's now stands. There is no early *Vita* of Patrick, and almost all the documents claiming to be from his hand, or those of his disciples, have been shown to be spurious. Two later works, Prosper's *Chronicle* and the *Annals of Ulster*, say that, in AD 431, Pope Celestine sent Palladius as bishop to Ireland (implying that a rudimentary Christian community already existed there), and the *Annals* add that Patrick followed the next year. Two Latin letters dating from this period, the so-called *Confession* and the *Letter to the Soldiers of Coroticus*, state categorically that they are written by Patrick. The first informs us that Patrick was a member of a Romanized British family, presumably living in Pembrokeshire or elsewhere in South Wales, and that at the age of sixteen he was carried off to Ireland as a slave by pirates; after spending six years there he escaped, but later he returned there, as an act of piety, to help the process of evangelization.

What seems to have happened is that, in the fifth century, possibly even before, the weakening of Roman power led to Irish penetration of South Wales, especially Pembrokeshire. The Romans, as was their custom, established a friendly, semi-civilized Irish tribe there, to protect the coast from barbarous Irish pirates. It thus became a little Irish kingdom, later called Dyfed, with an Irish-speaking ruling class, of which Patrick was a member. It was the activity of this class, which was Christianized as well as (to some extent) Romanized, which led to the spread of Christianity to Ireland, and later to Scotland. Neither the sixth-century Welsh monk Gildas, nor the early-eighth-century Northumbrian Bede – the most systematic and reliable of the ecclesiastical historians – mentions Patrick. Instead, his cult was promoted from Ireland itself, especially by the triumphant Ui Neill (or O'Neill) dynasty, which founded at Tara the myth of an ancient over-lordship, or high kingship, of Ireland, conquered Ulster, and then, from about AD 637, crossed into Argyll. One of the O'Neills was St Colomba, and it was he who founded the great monastic establishment of Iona, from which Christianity penetrated east into Scotland, and then turned south into the emerging Northumbrian kingdom. The story is complex, and the evidence fragmentary; but it would seem that Celtic Christianity moved in a gigantic arc along the western fringes of the British Isles – from Wales to Ireland, from Ireland to Scotland, from Scotland to northern England.

This Christianity was Roman, in the sense that its ultimate inspiration came from Rome, and it recognized bishops. After

The twelfth-century Welsh historian, Geraldus Cambrensis, who chronicled the early history of St David's see.

all, as St Patrick assures us, he was Roman-trained himself. But in its externals and organization it had little in common with the Roman church of the Continent, which was city-orientated, based on urban bishoprics, and a strict hierarchy – the spiritual counterpart of the empire. In the Celtic areas there was no Roman tradition, no cities or even towns, and no means to create a centralized system of command. Instead, in these remote parts, where Christian communities were widely scattered and often lost contact with each other for years, even decades, there was a strong tendency to adopt monastic forms of organization and worship. These originated in the deserts of Egypt, Syria and Mesopotamia, where Christian ascetics had settled in tiny communities or even as solitaries, abandoning worldly rank and possessions, families, even in some cases their names (Eugippius tells us in his life of St Severinus that, to the end of his life, he never revealed his name).

14

The ascetic or monastic movement spread from the eastern Mediterranean to Provence, and then through Gaul to the Celtic fringes. There, it was enthusiastically adopted, for it was congenial to the Celtic culture and well adapted to its geography.

This is how the foundation of St David's came into being. The twelfth-century Welsh historian, Geraldus Cambrensis, notes that the site is exposed both to the elements and to pirate raids, but he says that this was deliberate, for its founders were hermits – indeed, there were similar, but smaller, foundations on rocky or island sites around the Pembrokeshire coast. The little Irish kingdom which existed in the days of St Patrick, he says, was called Demetia, and St David's itself Menevia; but it was conquered by the Welsh-speaking house of Powys from North Wales, and then, he adds, the Bishop, Dubricius, resigned the see to David, who must have been a member of the royal line of Powys. In Welsh, David is Dewi; the old Menevia was called after him, and became known as Tydadewi, the House of David. Whether St David is actually buried in the cathedral we cannot know for sure, but it seems likely. In Geraldus's time they believed it to be so. The old shrine of St David in the cathedral was demolished in the iconoclastic sixteenth century, but a stone base, dating from about 1275, remains and this was presumably erected on the site of an earlier altar. In 1866, some bones were found in a casket beneath the altar, and this would be the most likely place for the monks to have buried their saint.

Geraldus's account stresses the great antiquity of the see; he lists the names of twenty-five bishops who followed David, including the learned Bishop Asser, who went to the court of King Alfred of Wessex, and wrote his life-story. But he also laments the fact that the importance of St David's had declined; he calls it 'the head, and in times past the metropolitan city, of Wales, though now, alas, keeping more of the name than of the reality'. This decline reflected the extinction of the specific Celtic form of Christianity, which by the twelfth century was complete. The papacy, indeed, had always been hostile to a Church organized on monastic, or hermitical, lines, rather than urban bishoprics reporting directly to Rome. As long ago as AD 428, in a famous letter addressed to the Bishops of Vienne and Narbonne, Pope Celestine had deplored the tendency to give bishoprics to monks, whom he called 'wanderers and strangers', and whose ascetic habits and weird appearance detracted from the dignity of a Church which sought to impress the world by the majesty of its temporalities.

those who have not grown up in the church act contrary to the church's usages . . . coming from other customs they have brought their traditional ways with them . . . clad in a cloak and a girdle round their loins . . . Such a practice may perhaps be followed . . . by those who dwell in remote places and pass their lives far from their fellow men. But why should they dress in this way in the churches of God, changing the uses of so many years, of such great prelates, for another habit?

As a matter of policy, the popes were anxious to abolish this disorderly approach to the faith even 'in remote places', and they proceeded to do so as soon as they had the power. The Celtic church emerged, and survived, only because Rome could not physically get at it. Contact had been lost around AD 450, and so when the vexed controversy surrounding the date of Easter was settled seven years later, news did not reach the Celtic Christian communities of the British Isles, which continued to observe the earlier calculations. When Rome again began to penetrate Britain, or England as it now was, from the south-east, the question of Easter assumed an importance well beyond its intrinsic merits. Were the native churches to accept the authority of Rome in all things, down to the details of the calendar, the form of tonsures, vestments and liturgy, or were they to maintain their own traditions, sanctified by the practices of their founder-saints and martyrs? What was really at issue was the organization of the Church: on the one hand, an urban episcopate, highly secular in outlook, and tightly controlled by the papacy; on the other, a collection of semi- or wholly-independent monastic communities. From the early seventh century, the Irish churches began to accept the rulings of Rome; by 636 all southern Ireland had joined the new order. Northumbria opted for Rome in 663, at the famous Synod of Whitby. A few years later, Adamnam, Abbot of Iona, accepted the Roman Easter, and the monks of Iona themselves capitulated in 716. In Wales, Cornwall and Brittany the resistance was more prolonged; but in 818, Abbot Matmonoc of the leading Breton monastery at Landevennec, complied with the plea of King Louis the Pious to bow to the pope, and Cornwall and South Wales followed suit. By the time Bishop Asser of St David's came to Alfred's court, his diocese had been Romanized, and while monasteries were allowed to continue, their inmates had to observe the centrally-controlled, and papally organized, Rule of St Benedict. Perhaps this was one reason Asser sought a career in England. The location of St David's made sense in terms of the Celtic church. But under the organized authority of Rome, it had less to offer an ambitious cleric.

Indeed, the wonder is that St David's survived at all as an episcopal see. It was saved, beyond doubt, by its possession of St David's bones. It must have been a place of pilgrimage since very early times. In this respect its remoteness was an advantage: a pilgrim gained more merit if his journey was long and hazardous. About 1120 it was formally raised to the status of a place of pilgrimage by Pope Calixtus II, who laid down – using the minute exactness beloved of Medieval man – that a visit to St David's shrine was worth, in spiritual remission of sin, precisely half of one to Rome itself. So the place survived, even to some extent flourished. Geraldus tells us that Henry II went on a pilgrimage there, no doubt travelling by sea, the usual method: there is a late Medieval carving on a misericord in the cathedral showing a boatload of pilgrims on the way, one of them being

Above Pope Callixtus II, who, in the early twelfth century, raised St David's to the status of a place of pilgrimage.

violently seasick. Geraldus knew this part of the world well: he was born in Pembrokeshire, on the south side, in the castle of Manorbia, whose superb setting in a valley by the sea – still untouched by modern 'improvements' – he describes in an eloquent passage. He himself had a distant connection with Henry II, since his grandmother Nesta, daughter of the Prince Rhys ap Twewdwr, had once been Henry's mistress. He was anxious for Henry to make him Bishop of St David's, but the king consistently refused, and so was made the subject of a venomous character-sketch in Geraldus's writings. The fact that Geraldus wanted St David's is interesting: he was well-born, able, ambitious, a scholar. So the see must have been worth having.

No doubt it was the contributions of pilgrims which made possible the rebuilding of the cathedral, the third we know to have existed on the site. It was being constructed when Geraldus visited St David's in 1188, but progress was intermittent, and it was not actually finished until 1522. In the meantime, Henry de Gower, the richest and most vigorous of the medieval bishops of St David's, had built the Tower Gate and the walls that enclose the precinct, and in the 1340s he had erected a fine palace. St David's might have expected a revival when the Tudors made their way to the forefront of English politics. Owen Tudor claimed descent from the same Welsh royal line as Geraldus, though he was a person of little substance, a mere attendant at Henry V's court. After the king's death, he attached himself to his widow, Katherine of France, and later married her secretly. This, of course, did not give their son, Edmund, any claim to the throne, but it brought him into prominence, and he was given the wardship of Margaret Beaufort, one of the Plantagenet claimants. He married this girl, aged thirteen, as soon as she was capable of consummating the sexual act – just in time, as it happened, for he was already dead when she gave birth to an heir, the future Henry VII. Edmund was buried in St David's, where his tomb can still be seen, and it was not far away, at Milford Haven, that his son landed from France to claim the

Right The Gothic vaulting and tracery of the ceiling, dating from the later Middle Ages.

throne he won at Bosworth Field. But Henry VII never showed
much interest in Wales. The truth is, though his grandfather,
Owen, was wholly Welsh, he himself had French, Bavarian and a
great deal of English blood, and he certainly considered himself
an Englishman – there is no evidence he spoke the Welsh language.
His son, Henry VIII, far from giving Wales an independent status,
incorporated the principality in the English system of law and
government, forbad the use of Welsh in the courts, and administered the territory through the English-dominated Council of the
Marches of Wales, which sat in Ludlow. Queen Elizabeth, it is
true, had several Welsh attendants, and the family of her greatest
minister, William Cecil, Lord Burghley, came from the Welsh
Borders. But she never showed the slightest interest in Wales,
never visited it, and pooh-poohed the efforts of Sir Henry Sidney,
who was President of the Council of the Marches for most of
her reign, to raise Welsh living standards; Sir Henry was, she
complained, 'a most expensive servant'.

Indeed, St David's suffered greatly in Tudor times. William
Barlow, a reforming crony of Henry VIII, who was made bishop
in 1536, regarded St David's as a wholly unsuitable place from
which to run what was, and still is, a huge diocese. He was a
very angular fellow, and quarrelled violently with his chapter.
What was at issue was his opposition to 'Romish' practices, such
as relics, statues, indulgences – above all, the pilgrimages which
had made St David's famous, and brought it what wealth it
possessed. He disliked the atmosphere of St David's so much that
he wanted to transfer the see to Carmarthen, and leave the
cathedral to decay. During his time the shrine was stripped of
many of its valuables, and to mark his hatred of the place he tore
the lead off the palace roof – an outrage from which it has never
recovered: both the palace and the nearby College of St Mary are
now ruins. His critics accused Barlow of selling the lead to
provide dowries for his five daughters, all of whom married
bishops (his only son became an archdeacon). Certainly, like
many bishops of the period, both Reformers and Catholics, he
alienated some of the property of the see to line his own pockets.
But Barlow was undoubtedly sincere in his views, and his plan to
reorganize the diocese was a sensible one. He realized that, since
the Welsh bishops were almost invariably English-born and
English-speaking, the local population was becoming alienated
from the established Church. Barlow also had the distinction of
perpetuating the 'Apostolic Succession' in the Anglican hierarchy,
for it was he who consecrated Archbishop Matthew Parker of
Canterbury, the first primate of the new Anglican church brought
into being by Parliament in the first year of Elizabeth. Roman
Catholic efforts to demonstrate that Barlow himself was not
canonically consecrated – thus invalidating all Anglican
orders since Parker's appointment – have not stood the test of
historical research.

Unfortunately, the efforts of Reformers to create a Welsh-speaking episcopate and higher clergy in Wales were unsuccessful until it was too late. Under Elizabeth, the Bible was translated into Welsh, but St David's continued to be treated as merely a step on the episcopal ladder for ambitious English clergymen, such as Laud who held the see for five years in the 1620s. Such transitory incumbents tended to diminish the property of the see still further, and since the income from pilgrims had dried up, there was scarcely enough money to maintain the cathedral services, let alone attract sufficient men of ability to the diocese. Of the forty bishops of St David's from 1505 to 1874, only five were Welsh, and twenty were translated to other sees. In the seventeenth and eighteenth centuries the cathedral was much neglected, and in 1797 the lead was taken off its roof to be melted down into bullets to supply the local yeomanry, hastily marshalled to repel

Casket containing supposed relics of St David.

A misericord in the Cathedral, with carved figures of seasick pilgrims travelling to St David's Shrine.

a French landing on the north Pembrokeshire coast. The cathedral was eventually restored, and in time the Church of Wales was reorganized and disestablished. But by then the damage was done: the bulk of the Welsh people had moved to Methodism and Nonconformity, and St David's today cannot claim to be the spiritual shrine of a living people.

What it is, essentially, is a memorial to a very distant church indeed – a church which flourished on both sides of the Irish Sea during one of the darkest periods in recorded history, and which embodied a vibrant and appealing culture which has likewise vanished. There is no place in Britain – except perhaps Iona itself – which conveys to the visitor so powerfully an impression of this lost church and culture, a civilization transmitted by pious, solitary, wild-eyed men, dressed in rough hides and coarse-woven cloth, travelling in tiny boats, learned in Latin and the scriptures, skilled illuminators and sculptors, musicians and poets; men whose natural and beloved habitat were the grey stones and cliffs, the wildly changing skies, the tumultuous seas and the soft, rain-washed moors of these desolate lands on the rim of the world.

23

2 ST ANDREWS
Grammar Dogma and Golf

IF GLENCOE epitomizes the Celtic spirit of the Scottish Highlands, St Andrews is the citadel of the Lowlands culture. Andrew Lang, who studied at its ancient university, called it 'a little city, worn and grey'. And that is exactly what it is, little, undoubtedly, even today, but with the unmistakable dignity and appearance of a city which has made a long contribution to history. From the top of St Rule's tower, over one hundred feet up – all that survives of a fine Norman-Romanesque church – you look down on the three principal streets, North Street, Market Street and South Street, broad avenues, almost boulevards, which converge in a thoroughly satisfying and logical manner near the ruins of the cathedral. Beyond is the little harbour; up the sea-shore are the battered remnants of the archiepiscopal castle and palace. St Andrews is certainly worn, and grey too: not merely by virtue of its stones, but by the greyness of the Tay to the north, of the Firth of Forth to the south, and of the cold North Sea which stretches to the east. Lang added: 'a haunted town it is to me', and it is not hard to see what he meant, for many ghosts from the past have the right to walk its streets.

There is a tale that St Regulus was shipwrecked at this place in the fourth century, carrying in his baggage the relics of St Andrew, the gentle brother of Simon Peter. This seems improbable, but the identification of the settlement with St Andrew goes back to the eighth century, at a time when Christianity was spreading rapidly up the east coasts of Britain, carried forward from one fishing-village to another by itinerant monks in small open boats. Some of these monastic sea-colonies became flourishing centres of civilization, as at Jarrow and Lindisfarne, with copious libraries, schools of plain-chant and illuminated manuscripts, and regular contacts with the cities of Merovingian France, and even Rome. The settlement at St Andrews was doubtless a more primitive affair, but its geographical position gave it advantages in a burgeoning culture whose communications were essentially maritime. It soon became a bishopric, and by the tenth century the seat of the Christian primacy of Scotland.

Cardinal Beaton, rich and dissolute, archetype of the Renaissance Prince-bishop of the old order.

The spread of the church and the spread of a written, ordered culture in Scotland are inseparable. When, in the wake of the Norman conquest of England, the Hildebrandine reforms and the feudal organization of land and lordship penetrated into the Scottish lowlands, St Andrews became a centre where these new notions were eagerly implanted, and from which they were rapidly propagated. The new society was rural in the sense that it was replacing a pastoral economy by settled agriculture, and tribal arrangements by written contracts of service, and land-deeds; but it was also urban, based upon walled burghs where a form of English was spoken and where a regular coinage circulated. Early in the twelfth century, the monastic establishment at St Andrews was reorganized as a priory of the Canons Regular of St Augustine, and by 1160 they had begun to replace an older church by what was to be the largest cathedral in Scotland. The fact that it was the repository of the supposed remains of St Andrew reinforced its importance when the saint was identified with the cause of Scottish nationalism and the growing consciousness of Scotland as an independent and coherent kingdom. In 1320, six years after the great victory of

26

Bannockburn, the barons of Scotland met at Arbroath and swore an oath that the Scottish race had originally come to Scotland, via Ireland, from Scithia, where they had been evangelized by Andrew – whom God had 'appointed to be our leader and patron saint for ever'.

In the Middle Ages, then, St Andrews was a rich and important episcopal burgh, by the somewhat meagre standards of the Scottish kingdom. In 1410, university teachers and students began to gather there, in the College of St Mary's, established by the bishop. Another college, St Salvator's, was added forty years later and a third, St Leonards, in 1512. Indeed, it was during the early sixteenth century that St Andrews reached the height of its prosperity. The great cathedral and the priory buildings were surrounded by a fine wall built in 1516 – a mile in circumference, four feet thick, twenty feet high, and pierced by three gateways (two of which still stand). The old college of St Mary's was rebuilt and embellished, and the cathedral itself, with its multiple altars, shrines, reliquaries, roods and wall-paintings, statues and gold and silver plate, was a rich depository of the artifacts of late medieval Christendom, the combined Canterbury and Westminster Abbey of Scotland. The see had been raised to an archbishopric in 1472 and in the nearby castle-palace the archbishops lived in some grandeur, dispensing a power which was terrestrial as well as sacred, and enforcing the canon law with a salutary degree of terror.

St Andrews, as the ecclesiastical capital of Scotland, was inevitably both a centre of the corruption which marked the Medieval church in its decadence, and a hotbed of Reformers. Scotland was slow to receive the new humanist culture of the Renaissance, but St Andrews, with its university, was quickly drawn into the theological disputes which radiated from Germany in the early sixteenth century. It had long been a place where church discipline had been most fiercely asserted. One of the sea-towers of the archbishop's castle had a peculiarly unpleasant dungeon for spiritual offenders. Prisons throughout Scotland were usually underground, often carved out of solid rock: they were known, in fact, as 'pits'. At St Andrews, the pit was bottle-shaped, with rock walls twenty-five feet deep. It was sixteen feet wide at the bottom, and the only access was a seven-foot aperture at the top. Looking at it today, it is hard to imagine how anyone could long have survived in such a place: perhaps they were not meant to.

The church burned as well as imprisoned. At St Andrews in 1407 one John Risby suffered at the stake, followed by the Bohemian heretic, John Crawar in 1433. When the Reformation swept northern Europe, Church persecution became more systematic in Scotland, especially under the regime of David Beaton, who became Archbishop of St Andrews in succession to his uncle James. Beaton was the archetype of the Renaissance prince-bishop of the old order: a Wolsey of the north, straddling

Opposite Glencoe: the most dramatic of the Highland glens.

the clerical and secular worlds. As the noble-born, well-connected nephew of the primate, he accumulated benefices from childhood; he became a favourite of King James v and ambassador to France, where he added a bishopric and other posts to his collection of church honours. Beaton, like his uncle, was both a rich and a dissolute man: he had several bastards, including a daughter whom he married to the Master of Crawford with the princely dowry of 4,000 marks (nearly £3,000 sterling). He was also a passionate upholder of the papacy, and its political and military underpinning, the Franco–Scottish connection, which came to the centre of politics when Henry viii of England broke with Rome.

Even in the lifetime of his uncle, as co-adjutor of the see, Beaton controlled the Scottish church, a position reinforced by his appointment as papal legate, and Chancellor of the Scottish kingdom. When, in the 1520s, criticism of the church authorities became widespread in Scotland, Beaton acted with great cruelty and ruthlessness. He had four humble men hanged for, among other offences, breaking the abstinence laws by eating a goose on Friday. Heretics were burned in Edinburgh and Perth. Although he had been to the university himself, Beaton held the St Andrews colleges in great suspicion – especially St Leonard's: 'to have drunk at St Leonard's well' meant to have imbibed the doctrines of the reformers. In 1528 he had Patrick Hamilton burnt alive in front of St Salvator's. Hamilton was a man of some importance, of royal descent and a former abbot: the religion he professed appears to have been a mild Lutheranism, such as was shared by a growing number of the Scots nobility, and his horrible death created a sensation. Beaton was advised, in future, to kill his victims in some dark cellar, 'for the reek of Maister Patrik Hammyltoun has infested as many as it blew upon'. In fact, partly as a result of the persecution, the Reformist movement was passing from the hands of those who sought merely to correct flagrant abuses in the Church to those who wanted a wholly new system of ecclesiastical organization and a faith based solely on the Bible – what would soon be called Calvinism or Presbyterianism. A harbinger of the more radical movement was George Wishart who, in the early 1540s, preached to growing congregations of nobles and townsmen. Beaton, now a cardinal, managed to get his hands on Wishart by an act of treachery, tried and convicted him for heresy in St Andrew's Cathedral, and burnt him at the stake in front of the castle. The cardinal showed his contempt for the mob by watching the proceedings, at his ease, from his bedroom window high in the castle walls; but he had the cannon on the battlements loaded and trained on the scaffold, to prevent any rescue attempt.

Beaton was a great builder and patron of the arts; and this was his undoing. Having rebuilt St Mary's, he was now engaged on making his castle more splendid, and a hundred masons entered daily to carry on the work. On 28 May 1546, two months

after the Wishart burning, a group of sixteen conspirators led by Norman Leslie, son of the Earl of Rothes, gained access to the castle by pretending to be labourers and overcame the guards. Beaton was in his bedroom and when he heard the uproar he had the door barred and called for his two-handed sword. But Leslie threatened to burn him alive and Beaton allowed the door to be opened. He was stabbed to death on his knees, calling out: 'Fie, fie, I am a priest – all's gone.' His body, wrapped in a sheet, was hung out of the window from which he had watched Wishart die, and afterwards, covered in salt, it was thrown into the bottle-dungeon, 'to await,' as John Knox later recorded in his *History of the Reformation in Scotland*, 'what exsequies his brethren the bishops would prepare for him.'

Knox was not present on this occasion, though he defended the murder. After all, had not Beaton, only a few years before, had a

Above John Knox, greatest of the Scottish Calvinists. His will-power and eloquence gave Scotland her new national faith.

Left George Wishart, the Scottish reformer who was burnt at the stake on the orders of Cardinal Beaton in 1546.

Opposite St Andrew's University, the third British University founded in the fifteenth century.

Inverary Castle: headquarters
of the Campbells, the
architects of the Glencoe
Massacre.

recalcitrant monk murdered at St Andrews and hurled over the
sea-wall? Knox was a pupil and disciple of Wishart, another
alumnus of St Andrews; he had proudly carried a great sword in
front of his master when he processed to church to preach. At
Easter 1547, aged twenty-three, Knox took shelter with the
Protestant conspirators, who were still holding out in the castle.
But two months later, a French fleet summoned on behalf of the
'ould alliance', compelled it to surrender, and Knox, with others,
was sent to penal servitude in the French galleys. If Knox had died
in the galleys as most convicts did, the history of Scotland, and of
St Andrews in particular, might have been very different. There
was a popular undercurrent for reform in Scotland, and the
faction-politics of the nobility assured it substantial support in
high places; even so, without Knox's unrelenting eloquence and
will-power, it is questionable whether Calvinism could have
established itself, in effect, as the national faith; the Scots might
have turned to that milder blend of reform which, farther south,
became Anglicanism. As it was, Knox's friends secured his release
after eighteen months; and when, a decade later, England opted
for the Elizabethan settlement in religion, he felt it both safe and
opportune to return home. He reached Scotland on 2 May 1559
and within days he was preaching at Perth, exhorting his massed
congregations to rise up against the monkish rule of the Church,
smash the 'instruments of idolatry', expel the bishops, and
appoint 'Godly preachers'. This was the beginning of a mass-
movement. Early in June he came to St Andrews, giving his first
sermon in the church of the Holy Trinity, and thereafter, on three
successive days, in the cathedral, to the text of 'Christ cleansing
the temple'. Whether Knox actually ordered the people to sack
the churches is questionable; but he did nothing to stop the burning of roods and statues, the lootings of shrines and reliquaries,
and the defacing of paintings and monuments which followed.
Thus Scotland lost her treasures of Medieval ecclesiastical art,
notably at St Andrews itself; and the Reformation was firmly
established when the French occupying forces surrendered the
following year.

The new spiritual regime retained the ferocity of its predeces-
sor. Knox himself took a personal and vigorous part in at least
one witchcraft trial at St Andrews. The Presbyterian discipline
insisted that the 'elect' element among the faithful – preachers
and elders – had a God-given right to supervise the private lives
of the entire congregation, and chastise backsliders. Thus
Scotland endured a form of theocracy which lasted until the Act
of Union. There was a marked tendency to concentrate upon
sexual offences. Adultery might be punished by death, and sometimes was. Fornicators were made to sit on the Stool of Repent-
ence, and preached at in front of the entire congregation for six
successive weeks; since pregnancy could not be concealed, while
seducers were difficult to identify or convict, women were the
chief sufferers – though male homosexuals were liable to be

Knox preaching
before Mary Queen
of Scots and the
Lords of the
Congregation, from
the famous painting
by Sir David Wilkie.

burnt, roped together. English visitors deplored the fanaticism of the Scots: 'Under the sun,' wrote one ambassador, 'live not more beastly and unreasonable people than here be of all degrees.' It was noted that the drive to stamp out sexual immorality was conducted at the expense of perhaps more important matters. Between 1560 and 1600 the court of kirk-session at St Andrews judged over one thousand cases of sexual crime, more than one a fortnight; only one prosecution for usury is recorded during the same period.

In one respect, Knox was unjustly blamed: he did not pull down St Andrews cathedral itself, though his adherents certainly despoiled it. The Presbyterians faced a real difficulty in that they did not know what to do with the fabrics of the cathedrals. They acknowledged no bishops or archbishops, monks or chapters; they had adequate churches for the needs of their congregations; what spiritual purpose, then, could these costly buildings serve? In some places, as at Dornoch, the cathedral became a mere parish kirk, and is now classified as a 'Historic Church' of the established Church of Scotland. At St Andrews, it mouldered. During the troubled period of the Commonwealth, in the 1640s and 1650s, some of its stones were taken by authority to repair the castle. Thus encouraged, the townsfolk followed suit and the place became a ruin, like the old abbeys of England. What is more surprising is that the Presbyterians failed to reinforce the university status of the town, for in general they were earnest educators, and gave to Scotland what is in essence the finest system of public education in Europe. Perhaps St Andrews, with its suspect aura as the former capital of Catholic Scotland, was thought unsuitable for higher studies; at all events, the university decayed and slumbered, though it never ceased to carry out its functions, after a fashion.

The loss of status as a cathedral city and the decline of scholastic life inevitably infected the town. In the seventeenth and eighteenth centuries, St Andrews was a melancholy place. From a description of 1697, we learn that the streets were 'filled with dunghills, and extremely noisesome, especially on account of the herring guts exposed on them'. There was 'not a foot of pavement in any of the streets', and 'Cows and pigs graze in front of the colleges'. In the mid-eighteenth century an effort was made to save the university by consolidation: St Salvator's and St Leonard's were amalgamated into the United College for Arts and Science, while St Mary's continued to house the theological faculty. The buildings of St Leonard's passed into private hands (before becoming, in more modern times, a girls' school).

It was at lodgings in St Leonard's, belonging to a university professor, Dr Watson, that Dr Samuel Johnson and James Boswell were accommodated when they visited St Andrews in 1773. They were pleased to get a good meal at an inn on their arrival and found their rooms at Dr Watson's, Boswell records, 'comfortable and genteel'; indeed they had no cause to complain of St Andrews hospitality, or of the deference with which the professors treated the 'Great Cham' of English letters. Johnson even found some words of praise for the university library, though he considered it did not merit the panegyrics of his hosts. But he was dismayed by the evident decline of the university as such. He thought it disgraceful that Scotland 'suffers its universities to moulder into dust'. There were only, he noted, about a hundred students; the parents of upper-class boys paid £15 a term, the lower orders £10, 'in which board, lodging and instruction are all included'. With such meagre resources, no wonder learning did not flourish: the place filled him 'with mournful images and ineffectual wishes'.

As for the cathedral, he paced about its crumbling stones with his hat off, lost in thought. Afterwards, he related how he had 'surveyed the ruins of ancient magnificence, of which even the ruins cannot long be visible, unless some care be taken to preserve them; where is the pleasure of preserving such mournful memorials . . . every man carried away the stones who fancied he wanted them'. Here was 'the silence and solitude of inactive indigence and gloomy depopulation'. Boswell records that, when he saw the ruins, Johnson was 'affected with a strong indignation' and fulminated against John Knox, whom he supposed responsible. When Boswell asked where Knox was buried, Johnson burst out: 'I hope in the highway. I have been looking at his *reformation*.' He thought that 'differing from a man in doctrine was no reason why you should pull his house about his ears'. His attention was drawn to a ruined steeple, in a dangerous condition. Johnson opposed the suggestion that it should be demolished, for it might, he argued, collapse of its own accord and 'fall on some of the posterity of John Knox – and no great matter'. At that point dinner was announced. 'Aye, aye,' concluded Johnson, 'amidst all these sorrowful scenes, I have no objection to dinner.'

Less than a century before Johnson's visit, the final downfall of episcopacy in Scotland – or rather of the Stuarts' attempts to reimpose it as the dominant ecclesiastical form – had been signalized by the brutal murder of Archbishop Sharp of St Andrews, on 3 May 1679. He was in his coach crossing Magus Moor, three miles from the town, when he was surprised by a militant mob of Presbyterian zealots, forced to get out, repeatedly stabbed, and died in the arms of his daughter who was travelling with him. Boswell and Johnson did not visit the little cairn, in a grove of trees, which marks the spot of this atrocity; nor, for that matter, did they see the memorial to the Protestant martyrs, on the outskirts of the town; but they saw Sharp's marble tomb in Holy Trinity church, the most sumptuous in this part of Scotland.

Johnson evidently did not think much of the religious forms observed in St Andrews. He was surprised that the professors, at table, did not say a Latin grace and supplied the deficiency himself. Despite this, or perhaps because of it, the university seems to have had the reputation, a few years later, of employing too much

'Dr Johnson and I walked arm in arm up the High Street . . . As we marched along he grumbled in my ear "I smell you in the dark".'

'The contest began whilst my father was showing him his collection of medals . . .'

Four illustrations by Rowlandson of Johnson and Boswell's tour of Scotland. *Above left Walking up the High Street; below left The Contest at Auchinleck; above right Scottifying the Palate; below right The Recovery.*

'I bought some Speldings
fish . . . dried in the sun an
eaten by the Scots with
relish . . . he did not like i

'I walked with a sore hea
went into Dr Johnson's
room . . . and read the
epistle: "and be not drun
with wine." Some would
have taken this as a divin
interpretation.'

The death of Archbishop
Sharp in 1679, a stylized
nineteenth-century view.

Latin, rather than too little. In 1776, a student reading church history at St Andrews complained that, in three years, he had never heard a word from his professor, except in Latin. The university's courses were judged to be hopelessly old-fashioned, and the professors unadventurous or worse. The students continued to wear their red gowns, but otherwise were celebrated for their docility – not a symptom of a vigorous university life: 'any tendency to riot, or to dissipation,' noted the Revd John Adamson in 1793, 'is immediately checked.' The colleges expanded their numbers, but only slowly. In 1824 the *Gazetteer* wrote: 'It is a matter of deep regret that the number of students seldom averages more than two hundred.' This, too, at a time when the universities of Edinburgh and Glasgow were rightly famous and when Scottish scientists, doctors, economists and men of letters were astonishing and leading the world.

In 1842, Sir Hugh Lyon Playfair, a member of one of Scotland's greatest manufacturing and academic families, retired to St Andrews, got himself elected Provost, and proceeded to rehabilitate both the town and the university where his father had once been principal of the United College. The three main streets were rebuilt, in that impressive post-Regency classical style which is the architectural glory of urban Scotland, and the university began to acquire a reputation again. But Playfair's work and modern St Andrews would not have been possible without the town's reputation for a sport which the elders of previous generations had not only despised but frequently tried to suppress. If St Andrews was founded on religion, it was refounded on golf.

The earliest mention of golf in the Scottish records reflects the anxiety of the authorities to prevent people from playing it. Medieval governments loathed any form of community exercise not connected with archery and martial training – football, in particular, was legislated against in practically every country in western Europe, not only because it stopped villages from training at the butts, but because it frequently led to riots. In Scotland, the state regarded the repeated military victories of the English as principally due to superior skill at the longbow, and saw golf, or 'gowf', as a social evil just as insidious as football. Thus, in 1456, the Scots Parliament passed a statute commanding that 'fute ball and Golfe be utterly cryit downe, and nocht usit, and that the bowe merkis be made at ilka [every] paroche kirke a paire of buttis, and schutting be usit ilk Sunday'. This, and other similar prohibitions against golf, were wholly ineffective. By the end of the sixteenth century it would seem that the efforts of the government, both national and local, were concentrating rather on banning the game on Sundays: the magistrates at Edinburgh passed an ordinance to this effect in 1592.

The trouble was that golf, unlike football in either Scotland or England, attracted the patronage of the well-born as well as rustics and town-ruffians. Charles I was an enthusiastic golfer. It was while he was playing a round on the Leith links in 1641 that news came of the disastrous rebellion in Ireland. Whereupon, says a contemporary account, he threw down his clubs and 'returned in great agitation to Holyrood House' (no Francis Drake he!). Charles must have inherited the taste for the game from his father, for James I not only played in Scotland but brought his enthusiasm to England, founding the first English golf club at Blackheath in 1608. Indeed, he and his family found themselves supporting Sunday golf as a manifestation of episcopacy, against the absolute ban of the Presbyterians. Thus, during his reign, the Archbishop of St Andrews deliberately defied the kirk by openly playing on the sabbath.

Whether golf was first played at St Andrews the records give no indication. What is certain is that the St Andrews links, among the sand-dunes along the seashore north of the town, first gave the game something approaching its modern sophistication and hazards. To a greater or lesser degree, all artificially created courses, wherever they may be found in the world, strive to imitate the contours, the variety of texture, length and difficulty of each hole, the masterful uncertainty of the game, which at St Andrews are provided by nature. The Old Course at St Andrews is the perfect course, because it was there that the rules of the game sprang from the terrain itself, and where golf ceased to be a scrimmage with clubs and balls, and became an august drama of sand, turf, wind, skill and concentration. Scotsmen were solemnly

playing round the Old Course as early as the fifteenth century. The rules observed there became standard by the mid-eighteenth century, when the Royal and Ancient Club of St Andrews was established, in 1754, as the central arbiter of the game – somewhat earlier than the Marylebone Cricket Club, at Lords, came to dominate cricket. By the early nineteenth century golf was more important to the prosperity of St Andrews town than the church or the university. Indeed, the same issue of the *Gazetteer* which deplored the small numbers of students at St Andrews added that 'the only article manufactured for exportation is *golf balls* . . . About a dozen men are constantly at work. . . . The consumption of the town amounts to three hundred dozen balls annually. . . . A man makes about nine balls a day.'

In those days, gentlemen members of the golf club, among whom were included professors, played in red coats; 'those of a plebeian society' wore green. While the rigidities of dress gradually disappeared – to some extent, at least – the class niceties of

Left 'The Two MacDonalds', an eighteenth-century painting.

Above Mary Queen of Scots plays golf at St Andrews.

the game have remained, even, to some extent, in Scotland, the only country in the world where all classes play it. At St Andrews today there are four full-sized courses, as well as five putting greens, and a vast complex series of regulations governing the priorities of those who wish to play, women, Sundays, and other topics which invariably arise where men take sports seriously. There is also a curious museum of the sport at the Royal and Ancient clubhouse, in which gruesome implements from the primaeval ages of the game are cherished. Like other university towns, St Andrews is enjoying a second spring in our age; but it is unquestionably golf which gives it the sleek plumage of prosperity. Not, perhaps, the most dignified outcome for a city which once epitomized civilization in Scotland. But, then, is not golf a uniquely Scottish contribution, if not to civilization at least to the harmless pleasures of mankind? At St Andrews it has the status and dignity of a religion; and one which, unlike the creeds of Beaton and Knox, does not claim lives.

43

Glencoe, 'a fortress and a trap'.

3 GLENCOE

The Suicide of the Clans

GLENCOE is not the biggest, or the longest, or indeed the highest of the Highland glens, but in many ways it is the most magnificent – and certainly the most dramatic. The Glen proper is a mere nine miles long, as it follows the course of the rushing River Coe; then the valley continues for a further six miles, until it peters out in the vast wilderness of Rannoch Moor, which links the mountain structure of the West Coast of Scotland to the Central Highlands. To the west of the Glen are sea-lochs. To the north is the high mountain ridge of Aonach Eagach, dominated by the Pap of Glencoe (2,430 feet), and crossed at its eastern end by an ancient zig-zag track known as the Devil's Staircase. To the south are three sister-mountains, Beinn Fhada, Gearr Aonach and Aonach Dubh, and behind them two giant peaks, Bidean nam Bian (3,766 feet) and Stob Coire nam Lochan (3,657 feet); and farther east, to complete the array of mountain battlements, are two more 3,000-foot summits, the Two Shepherds of Etive, Buchaille Etive Beag, and Buchaille Etive Mor. Wild sea-lochs, high moors, cliff-faces of up to 1,200 feet, echoing ravines, and an almost unbroken ring of great peaks – on all sides Glencoe is surrounded by natural barriers. It is a fortress; and a trap. What makes the place so theatrical is the abruptness with which the valley ascends from sea-level to the realms of mountain desert. Even in high summer and in dazzling sunlight, the looming proximity of the precipices is oppressive; in midwinter, when the blizzards rage and sleet and mist magnify the cliff-faces, Glencoe is a scene of terror.

Yet in the seventeenth century such high glens supported a flourishing tribal society; indeed the clan system of the Highlands reached its apogee at this time, when the first penetration by the civilized south was bringing with it a trickle of wealth without, as yet, the legal and administrative customs which were to be fatal to the patriarchal way of life. Population was increasing. Glencoe itself supported nearly five hundred men, women and children, living off sheep and cattle (the latter their chief wealth), growing their own grain, distilling their whiskey, weaving and dyeing their plaids, making their brogues from the skins of deer, cutting timber and quarrying stone for their huts – a virtually self-supporting community, which bought its few luxuries by selling cattle (often stolen on raids). In the winter the clan lived on the valley-floor, scattered along the banks of the Coe. In the summer, they took their herds up to the high mountain pastures – as the Bakhtiari and other Persian tribes still do today – living in 'sheilings', which looked like stone-and-peat wigwams. Spring was the hardest time, as it is even now for the red deer, when food was scarce and the rigours of winter had lowered resistance. Then the clan was tempted to raid.

The clansmen of Glencoe (or most of them) were Macdonalds, a small, bastard branch of the great tribal confederation of the Macdonalds, the Lords of the Isles, who, besides the Hebrides, held Lochaber, Ardnamurchan and Kintyre on the mainland, and the Glens of Antrim in Ulster. In the fourteenth century, Angus Og of Islay, the first Lord of the Isles, the founder of what was in effect a second royal line of Scotland, had a bastard son, Iain Brach, who fought for Robert Bruce at Bannockburn. Lord Angus Og gave Glencoe to Iain, and thus his successors as chieftains of the Glen were called MacIain, though they were of course Macdonalds, like their followers. This was a military, though not a feudal, society. The chiefs reckoned their powers in terms of the number of fighting men they could lead into battle, so they charged low rents (calculated in units of black cattle) for their lands, and crowded on to them as many tenants as possible. There was grotesque overstocking, and many weak beasts. Between the chief and the tenants was an intermediate class of tacksmen, treated as gentlemen, though their children went without shoes, and whose sons formed a bodyguard to the chief – like the house-carls of Anglo-Saxon England. All the clansmen believed themselves to be ultimately descended from the same forbears as their chief. Thus he was their 'father', and his authority, though in theory absolute and often brutal, was also paternal. The chief administered customary tribal law and had power of 'pit and gallows'; he hanged clansmen who murdered or stole, or imprisoned them in his private dungeon. Sometimes he arranged marriages. But he could also be relied on to replace lost or diseased cattle, or to shelter impoverished tenants in his house. He and his tacksmen wore tartan trews and plaids, instead of the common kilts of the tenants, and buckled shoes instead of brogues. He had a two-storey house, and dined off linen and silver (kept in oak presses), and his drink was claret as well as whiskey.

The chief also had his bard, who composed and recited the clan's lays which were the history, literature and ideology of the tribe, the cultural force which supplied their cohesion, morale and dynamism. The head of the Glencoe Macdonalds in 1692, the MacIain, was Archibald Macdonald, twelfth chief of Clan Iain Arbrach, described by his bard as like a peacock's tail in his splendour and like a serpent's sting in his power to kill. He was, in fact, an unprincipled old ruffian, of unknown age but judged to be in his sixties, his flaming red hair now white, but six foot seven inches tall and still a formidable personality. As the young heir, he had fulfilled the custom of demonstrating his capacity to lead the clan by carrying out a successful cattle raid. He had led many raids since. In 1674 he had been briefly imprisoned in the lock-up at Inveraray, the one town on the whole of the West Coast; the charge was murder, and he was later accused of killing some of his own clansmen. But he had broken out of gaol, and he was not pursued back to his glen.

MacIain's tragedy was that the life-style he had inherited, and the social structure he sought to maintain, was under irresistible assault. Indeed, it had already, in theory, been abolished. The House of Stuart, Kings of Scotland, had de-throned the Lords of the Isles as long ago as 1493, and thus begun the process whereby feudalized, English-speaking and increasingly urban lowland Scotland undermined tribal society north and west of the Highland Line. The Lords overthrown, the life-rent of Glencoe went to the Stewarts of Appin, to whom the MacIains had to pay feu-duty. During the minority of Mary, Queen of Scots, the feudal

Loch Restil, one of the Lochs of Glencoe. This bleak land witnessed the massacre of the Macdonalds.

Buchaille Etive, now the centre of mountaineering in Scotland; once a region 'which five hundred ragged clansmen knew as home'.

lordship of Appin (and with it Glencoe) passed to the Campbell Earls of Argyll; and the Campbells, one of the two great expansionist or 'imperialist' clans of the Highlands, began to identify their interests in the seventeenth century with the forces of law and order, with a land-system based on title-deeds and regular proof of claim, with the English language of the courts, with the Presbyterian church, with settled agriculture, with the authority of central government, and with the 'English connection'. They stood for progress, civilization and the money-economy; the Macdonalds for the military anarchy of the past. The fact that MacIain had already been lodged, if briefly, in the Campbells' gaol at Inveraray, foreshadowed the future.

This conflict helps to explain the paradox which led the Macdonalds to identify their interests with the House of Stuart, another victim – though on the much grander scale of three kingdoms – of progressive forces. There was no historical reason why the Macdonalds, or any other struggling Highland clan, should love the Stuarts. The Stuarts had risen as administrative officers of the lowland state; then, as kings themselves, they had destroyed the lordship of the Isles; from Edinburgh, they had sought to extend the power of central government over the clans and their methods were as savage as they could make them. They were particularly hard on the smaller clans, like the Glencoe Macdonalds, who felt themselves forced to supplement a subsistence economy by raiding. Indeed, the Macdonalds were contemptuously known in court circles as the 'Gallows Herd'. The King's Council summoned clansmen to Edinburgh to answer for their crimes, and in default 'put them to the horn' (declared them outlaws). In graver cases the Council condemned a whole clan, issuing 'Letters of Fire and Sword' to a powerful local chief who could be relied upon to be loyal to the Crown in his own interests. The Stewarts of Appin had administered fire and sword against

48

the Macdonalds in the sixteenth century: the clan survived chiefly because it was impossible to track them down in the high pastures during the summer, and in winter lack of communications made large-scale military operations difficult. In 1603 the Stuarts had proscribed the whole of the McGregor clan; anyone was entitled to kill a McGregor like a beast, and appropriate his lands and property. Six years later, another commission of Fire and Sword went out against the Macdonalds: their chief and his son were killed, and their heads sent to the Council in a barrel. The chief beneficiaries of the Highland style of 'Indian fighting' were the Campbells, as indeed they were the chief victims of Macdonald raids. But there were periods of calm, and of compromise. The twelfth MacIain had married his son to a Campbell, and he had twice signed treaties of friendship with neighbouring Campbell branches. The Macdonalds varied their tribal strategy to suit the needs of the times; and sometimes they fought as mercenaries. But their basic conflict of interests with the Campbells was constant, as was their tendency to ally themselves with the forces resisting the spread of central government authority.

The downfall of the House of Stuart thus precipitated the climax. So long as the Stuarts dominated the lowlands, and reflected their interest, they were enemies of the clans; whenever they lost the lowlands, they were friends. Thus, during the Commonwealth, the Macdonalds fought for the stricken Stuart cause under Montrose. Again, in 1678, when Charles II's boss in Scotland, the Duke of Lauderdale, sought to impose episcopacy on the hostile lowlands, the Macdonalds and other clans joyfully responded to his appeal to come south to pillage and threaten the burghers and the lowland lairds. When the Earl of Argyll tried to raise the lowlands against James II in 1685, the Macdonalds again obeyed the royal command to terrorize Campbell domains. Once firmly in power, James turned against his mountain allies, issuing Letters of Fire and Sword against the Macdonalds only nine months before he lost his throne: he commanded 'all our good subjects' to unite 'in suppressing and rooting out the said barbarians and inhuman traitors'. But as soon as central authority passed to William III, the Macdonalds again made common cause with the Stuarts, fighting for them at Killikrankie. It was not James's Catholicism which appealed to them. The lowlanders called them Catholics chiefly as a term of abuse; there is no mention of priests or a church in Glencoe, and the truth is that in most of the Highlands there was then no form of settled religion, and pagan forms survived. What made the Macdonalds side with James was the combination of his physical weakness, and the strength of his hereditary title – and, equally potent, the fear of Campbell revenge.

The Stuart cause had collapsed in the Highlands at the end of 1689, and by the next year William III was establishing his authority on a permanent basis. The former Commonwealth fort at Lochinver, renamed Fort William, was rebuilt, and placed under an old Cromwellian soldier, Colonel John Hill. It dominated the sea approaches to Glencoe from the north; and the garrison of 1,000 men was supplemented by two Royal Naval vessels. The Crown thus had the power to subdue the disaffected clans by force, but Hill believed in conciliation. He thought, probably rightly, that the will of the Macdonalds and others to resist was not great. Their chief anxiety was that their desertion of James should not be dishonourable and they also sought – as part of a peaceful bargain – government funds to buy out their irksome feu-duties from the Campbells and other overlords, thus making their lands, for the first time, legal freeholds. There was some sympathy for this approach in government circles and £12,000 was allocated for the purpose, though there is no evidence it was ever used. But there was another school of thought, represented by Sir John Dalrymple, Master of Stair, who became Secretary of State for Scotland early in 1691. Stair was an extreme exponent of the 'English connection'. Indeed, he wanted to bring about a union of the two kingdoms, and lived to see it accomplished. He thought the wilder Highland tribes were incorrigible, and that a treaty with them would be meaningless. The year before he had delivered to William III his *Proposals Concerning the Highlanders*, which adumbrated the policy, adopted after 1745, of turning the Highlands into a man-power reservoir for regular troops. He wanted to terrorize the clans by making a bloody example of one of them, and he saw the Macdonalds of Glencoe – the most generally unpopular – as the likeliest candidates. This approach was not, and could not be, official policy, but it was clearly Stair's intention from the start.

But his trap was sprung by the folly of MacIain himself. Early in the summer of 1691, the Earl of Breadalbane, head of a junior Campbell branch, was authorized by the Crown to negotiate with the rebel chiefs. He arranged a three-month armistice on

30 June, and when this expired an agreement was reached under which the chieftains undertook to swear an oath of allegiance to William III, provided the ex-king James II – now living near Paris – released them from their allegiance to him. An emissary, Major Duncan Menzies, was sent to James's exiled court to obtain the necessary permission. In the meantime, 1 January 1692 was set as the absolute deadline by which the oaths must be sworn. All men who had been in arms against the Crown, or their authorized representatives, had to take the oath in the presence of the sheriffs of their counties before that date; otherwise they were outlaws, and the forces of the Crown were authorized to kill them without trial. Whether MacIain understood the conditions is not clear; he had refused to sign the armistice, and he may not have been present when they were laid down. But he can have had no doubt of the peril which faced him and his clan. Unfortunately, James II took three months to make up his mind whether or not to release the clans from their obligations, and it was not until 12 December that he allowed Menzies to leave court with his permission. The Major travelled back as fast as he could, reaching Edinburgh on 21 December; and he then made valiant efforts to get the news to the chiefs with all dispatch. Evidently he was successful, but the government was taking no chances. Men, supplies and ships were moved up to the Highlands. Fort William was reinforced on 29 December by four hundred men of the Argyll regiment, under Major Robert Duncanson. Most of their officers (and some of the men) were Campbells, who had suffered under Macdonald raids in 1674, 1685 and 1689; one, Captain Robert Campbell of Glenlyon, had twice been a victim and many of his household goods and cattle were now lodged in MacIain's enclave in Glencoe.

MacIain left his submission, in all the circumstances, culpably late, to the night of 30 December. Moreover, instead of going to Inveraray, to take the oath before the Sheriff, Sir Colin Campbell of Ardkinglas, he turned up at Fort William. Colonel Hill was furious at this folly, and apprehensive for the old man's safety. A few days before orders from Stair had reached the fort: 'It may be shortly we may have use of your garrison, for the winter time is the only season in which we are sure the Highlanders cannot escape us, nor carry their wives, bairns and cattle to the mountains. . . . Let me hear from you with the first whether you think that this is the proper season to maul them in the cold, long nights . . . [you] must be in readiness by the first of January.' Hill was aware that Stair deprecated his conciliatory attitude, and that the Secretary of State was in direct communication with the hard-line second in command at the fort, Colonel James Hamilton (though copies of Hamilton's instructions were sent to Hill). He was also aware that the four hundred Argylls were destined for any punitive raid up Glencoe. All he could do was to dispatch the old chief with all haste to the sheriff, and send a letter to the Council explaining that MacIain had made a mistake.

The only known portrait of Captain Robert Campbell, who received the instructions 'you are hereby ordered to fall upon the rebels, the Macdonalds of Glencoe, and to put all to the sword under seventy'.

MacIain now seems to have become thoroughly frightened, and he set off to find Sir Colin Campbell in appalling weather; by a series of misfortunes he was not able to take the oath until 6 January, and Campbell warned him it might not be accepted by the King and Council. His most prudent course would have been to travel on to Edinburgh and attend the Council in person to ensure that his surrender was valid. Instead, he followed his instincts, and returned to his lair in Glencoe.

When we are considering responsibility for the massacre, it is important to get the details right. There is no doubt that the Council was informed of the reasons for MacIain's late submission, though his name was removed by Crown lawyers from the official list of clan chiefs who had sworn. But there is also no doubt that William III approved of the plan to exterminate the Macdonalds, even if Stair did not explain to him the precise reasons for MacIain's failure to meet the deadline. On 11 January, William signed instructions to General Livingstone, Commander-in-Chief in Scotland, to proceed against those who had not taken the oath, and to 'cut off these obstinate rebels'. On 16 January, the King dispatched further orders to the General, which he signed at head and foot, as proof that he had read and approved them: 'If M'Kean of Glencoe, and that tribe', the letter reads, 'can be well separated from the rest, it will be a proper vindication to the public justice to extirpate that sept of thieves.' Thus William approved not merely the general policy of retribution, but Stair's particular plan to make an example of Glencoe.

Detailed instructions, lower down the chain of command, merely expanded these royal orders. Indeed, there was no possibility of misunderstanding. Stair wrote to General Livingstone: 'It's a great work of charity to be exact in rooting out that damnable sept, the worst in all the Highlands.' He told Hill: 'Let it be secret and sudden.' Livingstone, relaying his orders to Hamilton, commanded him not to 'trouble the government with prisoners'. On 1 February, Hamilton ordered two companies of Argylls, responsible to Major Duncanson, but under the actual command of Captain Robert Campbell, up to Glencoe, where they were quartered on MacIain and his clan. Therein, of course, lay the treachery. Campbell declined to stay in MacIain's house, as he did not relish the thought of eating off his own stolen silver. This might have alerted MacIain's suspicions. But he had been assured by Hill that, once he had sworn the oath, he was under the protection of the Fort William garrison. By this stage, Hill knew better; but he could not warn MacIain without risking a court martial, and he was an old, impoverished soldier who wished to end his days in government service.

In fact, all the actors in the drama were bound by unambiguous orders, which made it plain that the Macdonalds were to be killed without warning, without trial and without mercy. Hill got his final orders from Stair to carry out the plan on the evening of 11 February; he relayed them to Colonel Hamilton the next morning, and he, in turn, passed them on to Major Duncanson, who sent them to Captain Campbell on the spot. The words used in the various written orders are remarkably similar; the only deviation is that Duncanson, who was told to reinforce Campbell by blocking the sea-loch end of the Glen, put forward the operation, in his instructions to Campbell, from 7 am to 5 am on 13 February; this had the forseeable effect that he himself would not be present when the killing took place.

Otherwise all went according to plan, and to written order. The final instructions to Captain Campbell read: 'You are hereby ordered to fall upon the rebels, the Macdonalds of Glencoe, and to put all to the sword under seventy. You are to have a special care that the old fox and his sons do upon no account escape your hands. You are to secure all the avenues that no man escape. This you are to put in execution at five of the clock precisely.' In genocidal terms, the operation was not a complete success. There were about 150 Macdonalds of military age and they were defenceless, since they had buried their arms, fearing the soldiers would confiscate them. Some thirty-eight were killed, and this may include some women and children. They got the 'old fox', who was woken at exactly 5 am, and, believing his 'guests' were departing, was shot pulling on his trews, and bellowing for whiskey to speed their departure. His sons, however, escaped, as did several hundred others, though an undetermined number – chiefly the very old and the young – died quickly on the bare mountainside. A blizzard was raging at the time, and this helped members of the clan to escape once the alarm went up, though it froze some of them to death afterwards. And it may be that the redcoats had not much relish for their task. Of about 150 men in the two companies, three officers, one corporal and ten privates bore the name of Campbell, though others were members of the various Campbell clans; but many had no grudge against the Macdonalds, and certainly the pursuit was half-hearted. As a political act, however, the massacre succeeded. The Macdonalds of Glencoe were dispersed, and never were able to resume their depredations as a clan. The other disaffected clans took heed from the fearful example, and remained docile. To this extent Stair's strategy was justified.

Oddly enough, when news of the massacre got around – and Jacobite and French propaganda ensured that it did – the outrage was criticized less in the Highlands, whose fundamental rule of hospitality had been broken, than among the Presbyterians of the lowlands, where the 'sept of thieves' were most hated. The habit of the Highlanders was to seek revenge by the sword, and that was not possible. The lowlanders opposed through parliamentary forms, and that was easier. In 1695, the Scots Parliament set up a commission of inquiry. Its report provides us with the evidence set out above. It rightly identified Stair as 'the original cause of this unhappy business', and censured Robert Campbell as the chief agent. It laid down the principle that, even in the face of

Right The orders for the massacre.

You are hereby ordered to fall upon the Rebells, the
McDonalds of Glenco, and putt all to the sword und
sobenty. you are to have a speciall care that the ol
Fox and his sones doe upon no account escape you
hander you are to secure all the avenues that no
man escape. This you are to putt in execution
att fyve of the clock precisely; and by that time
or very shortly after it, I'le strive to be att you
with a stronger party: if I doe not come to you
att fyve, you are not to tary for me, butt to fall on
This is by the Kings speciall command, for the goo
safty of the Country, that these miscreants be cutt
off root and branch. See that this be putt in exec
tione without feid or favour, else you may expect t
dealt with as one not true to King nor Goverinment
nor a man fitt to carry Commissione in the Kings
service. Expecting you will not faill in the full
filling hereof, as you love your selfe, I subscribe
these with my hand att Balichobis feb: 12, 1692

For their Maties service.

To Capt
Robert Campbell
of Glenlyon.

Above The final act – the butchery of the clans at Culloden.

absolute orders, 'no command against the law of nature is binding', thus faintly foreshadowing the doctrine of the Nuremburg Trials. But it feared to censure the king, whose ultimate responsibility was proved by the documents. William not only took no action against Stair, but specifically exonerated him. Captain Campbell disappeared. No one was punished. The episode left bitter memories, which in time swelled into legends, but anger did not halt the course of history, the birth of the Union, or the destruction of Highland society.

Some of the clans were 'out' again during the abortive rising of 1715, and suffered in the years of sporadic fighting that followed. Their strongholds were reduced, among them the magnificent island castle of Eilean Donan, on Loch Long, which was smashed to rubble by naval bombardment in 1719; in the 1930s it was faithfully restored, and now delights tourists. In the 'Forty-Five', some of the clans came out once more, though more reluctantly; in many cases they responded only to the absolute commands of their chiefs, whose authority was crumbling fast. The clans were

heavily defeated at Culloden, and in the subsequent pursuit hundreds were butchered by the Duke of Cumberland's men. Some 3,471 were taken prisoner. Over 600 died in gaol, 121 were banished, 936 transported, and 120 – including four peers – were beheaded or hanged. Legislative steps were taken to destroy the clan system. The carrying of firearms, except by cattle drovers, was forbidden, Highland dress, bagpipes and bands were banned, the judicial powers of the chiefs were ended, and military tenures abolished. The estates of the rebellious chiefs were sequestered and administered by crown agents. Clansmen were recruited into the regular army, and posted overseas.

But, in any case, by the mid-eighteenth century, natural forces were already destroying the clan system as an economy and a way of life. The last inter-clan pitched battle had been fought in 1680. By 1700 the chiefs had ceased their ancient custom of fostering their children in the mountains, and were sending them to schools in Edinburgh. The bigger lairds encouraged settled husbandry and respect for the laws. The Duke of Argyll, the richest of them, wrote in 1756: 'I'm resolved to keep no tenants but such as will be peaceable and apply to industry.' Inveraray was rebuilt as a model township, followed by new urban centres like Oban, Ullapool, Beauly, Grantown and Tomintoul, which fostered a money economy. The cash-value of the natural resources of the Highlands – fish, timber, wool – rose steadily; the price of Highland cattle tripled in the forty years which followed the 'Forty-Five'. Potato planting took the edge off the fearful hunger which had driven the clansmen to theft. In 1773, after his famous Highland tour, Samuel Johnson pronounced the epitaph on the old system:

There was perhaps never any change of national manners so quick, so great and so general, as that which has operated in the Highlands by

Right Eilan Donan, the island castle which was destroyed in the suppression of the clans, and restored in the 1930s.

the last conquest and the subsequent laws. We came hither too late to see what we had expected – a people of peculiar appearance, and a system of antiquated life. The clans retain little now of their original character. Their ferocity of temper is softened, their military ardour is extinguished, their dignity of independence is suppressed, their contempt of government is subdued, and their reverence for their chiefs abated. Of what they had before the late conquest of their country there remains only their language and their poverty.

In fact, further and in some ways more tragic changes were to come. If the Highlanders had lost their independence and their social system by Johnson's day, they still had their glens. The population doubled in the second half of the eighteenth century; the value of the estates confiscated in 1745 rose from £12,000 to £80,000 in 1805. Military highways built by General Wade and his successors were followed by a new generation of civil trunk-roads, planned by that matchless engineer and architect Thomas Telford, and along them the products of the Highlands travelled south to market. But the economic depression which followed the

An eighteenth-century cartoon shows clansmen obeying orders from Parliament: these included the abolition of the traditional Highland dress.

end of the Napoleonic Wars hit all commodities except wool. Faced with hopelessly overcrowded glens, the utilitarian society of the early nineteenth century reacted with a mixture of paternalism and ruthlessness. The clans were encouraged to emigrate, or to move to new settlements on the coast, where attempts were made to establish industries. The glens were cleared, sometimes by force, and then restocked with superior brands of sheep, to the great profit of the chiefs, who watched the exodus of their followers dry-eyed. The clansmen migrated south, to the new industrial centres, or across the Atlantic, to Canada, the United States and Argentina. Those who remained turned to the fierce congregationalism of the many Presbyterian sects as an emotional substitute for the patriarchal society of the clan. In time, the huge popularity of Sir Walter Scott's novels led to a debased revival of the externals of the old society: the tartans, which were re-invented; the music of the pipes; the clan gatherings and dances. The 'Balmorality' epoch came; the lairds built themselves sham castles in Scots Baronial. The Highlands took on their modern aspect: glens empty except for carefully-preserved salmon and deer, and the hunting lodges of those who came to enjoy them. The population fell, the language disappeared.

Glencoe itself is now the chief centre of mountaineering in the Highlands. More young people come to scale the face of Buchaille Etive Mor than any other cliff in Scotland. The Forestry Commission, the Highlands and Islands Development Board, and the Hydro-Electric Board struggle to create local employment, to prevent the remaining Highlanders from becoming mere servants of the tourist trade. But in the islands the population is still falling, and on the east coast the battle is now being fought between the tourist interests and the ruthless demands of the North Sea gas-and-oil industry. Oil executives and wealthy weekenders compete to buy up the remaining crofts. The Gaelic society of the glens has gone for ever. When Lord Seafield, the last Chancellor of Scotland, sealed the documents of the Act of Union in 1707, he said to his clerk: 'Now there's an end to ane old song.' It takes an effort of imagination to hear its echoes in Glencoe today, though its streams and chasms and corries are just as delightful, and formidable, as when five-hundred ragged clansmen knew them as home.

4 WHITEHALL
Matrix of the Modern State

WHITEHALL is a striking example of the English habit of conceiving grandiose schemes and then, when it comes to the point,
settling for a comfortable, if incongruous, mixture of old and new.
In the early Middle Ages it became known simply as 'The Street',
because it was in fact the high road which linked the western exit
from the City of London, Temple Gate, to the great royal abbey
of Westminster and the palace which adjoined it. On either side
was farming-land, owned by the abbey. During the thirteenth
and fourteenth centuries, however, there was a tendency for the
rich and powerful to spread out from the western limits of the
City, and build themselves sumptuous town houses on the north
bank of the Thames. Thus the Dukes of Lancaster built the
Savoy Palace, the Palatine-Bishops of Durham added Durham
House, and in 1240 the Archbishop of York bought a chunk of
abbey land and built York Place, on a site just east of the present
Westminster Bridge. In the second and third decades of the
sixteenth century, the richest and most grandiose of all the Archbishops of York, Cardinal Wolsey, began to tear down the
old palace and rebuild it according to his more ample ideas.

We know little about the great archiepiscopal house, which was
never finished. It certainly included a hall, with turrets at each
corner; and it may be that the light colour of the stone gave
White hall its name. But by 1529 Wolsey was tottering to his fall.
Henry VIII had various reasons for destroying him, one of them
being his own housing problem. He had been casting envious
eyes on Wolsey's remarkable palace at Hampton Court, which he
preferred to his own at Richmond. Equally important, he needed
a house near Parliament to replace the royal apartments in
Westminster Palace, which had been gutted by fire in 1512.
Hitherto, he had been commuting from Greenwich, or using
Barnard's Castle, at the point where the Fleet River joined the
Thames; but this was old and inconvenient, and his intended new
wife, Anne Boleyn, complained she had no proper quarters
there. In 1530 he sent a message to the discredited Wolsey,
ordering him to hand over York Place. Wolsey, said his servant

and biographer Cavendish, protested that the house was the property of his see, 'which is none of mine'; but he none the less complied, bidding the messenger grimly 'to call to His Majesty's most gracious remembrance that there is both heaven and hell'.

Undeterred, Henry took over the property, and set on foot one of the most ambitious building programmes in the history of the capital. From the disestablished monasteries, he acquired 180 acres of land, stretching from the river to Charing Cross on the north, and what is now Buckingham Palace to the west. Most of it he laid

The King's Gate, which, with Holbein's Gate, marked the boundaries of 'The Street'. The gateways were part of the massive re-development undertaken by Henry VIII.

Holbein's drawing of the Minstrels' gallery in Whitehall Palace.

out as a park, and built St James's Palace as a semi-country retreat. At each end of The Street he built gatehouses, King's Gate and Holbein Gate (so called, not because Holbein designed it, but probably because he had quarters there). On the far side of The Street, overlooking St James's Park, he laid out what might be called an 'entertainment area': a cockpit, five indoor and outdoor tennis-courts, and above all a splendid tiltyard, with galleries and covered seating for spectators. (The bear-baiting pit, because of the smell, was at Paris Garden on the South Bank.) Whitehall Palace itself, of course, was on the river side of The Street, but it was linked to the tiltyard by a series of galleries which passed over The Street via the top storey of the Holbein Gate. To decorate this feature Henry inflicted a final insult on Wolsey, who had recently installed a magnificent carved gallery in his house at Eltham. On Henry's order, and in Wolsey's indignant presence, the gallery was dismantled and set up again at Whitehall; and this, said Cavendish, caused the Cardinal more sorrow than any other of the King's depredations.

Henry's building operations were conducted on a colossal scale all over south-east England. His Whitehall Palace, however, was never completed, at least according to his original plan. All that remains of it today is the wine-cellar, now bizarrely incorporated in the foundations of the new Ministry of Defence. In the time of his daughter, Elizabeth, it stretched over 23 acres, irregular and somewhat mean-looking without, magnificently decorated and furnished within. Its centrepiece was the great Privy Chamber, one whole wall adorned by a gigantic Holbein mural of Henry VIII and his family, the old King more than life-size, magnificent and ferocious. What it was like we can only judge by the cartoon

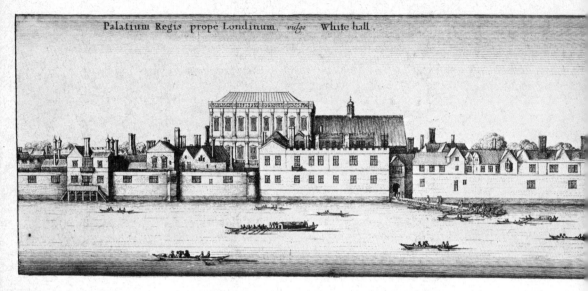

Palatium Regis prope Londinum, *vulgo* White hall.

Whitehall from the river, *c.* 1700. The Banqueting House rises above the surrounding buildings.

of the King, now in the National Portrait Gallery. But it was said to strike beholders 'with awe and even with dismay', and it was Elizabeth's habit, when receiving important visitors, to stand in front of it, to remind them whose daughter she was. Her own private quarters were spartan, for she liked to live simply when not on view; her bedroom had a solitary window, directly over the Thames, and a bathroom lined with mirrors next door. Whitehall Palace was not a private place. Not only did the main West-minster–London road go right through the middle, but the public was allowed to use the river-gatehouse, to attend outdoor sermons within the palace precincts, and, if suitably dressed, to walk in the main garden. This had a powerful fountain, which the younger courtiers liked to switch on suddenly when visitors were admiring it. The public could also attend the tilts, though they had to pay fivepence to get in, more than twice the cost of a theatre seat.

Neither Wolsey nor Henry VIII had succeeded in building the Whitehall they intended; Elizabeth was too prudent in money-matters; and James I disliked London too much to be bothered. But Charles I wanted to tear the whole place down, and create instead an architecturally unified palace, on the lines of Philip II's Escurial, near Madrid, or the Tuilleries in Paris. One of the more ramshackle aspects of Whitehall was a vast 'temporary' banqueting hall, built of canvas, wood and plaster, which in various guises had survived since 1581; it was painted inside to resemble a garden, and artificial fruit and vegetables hung from the roof, collecting dust, and shedding flakes of paint on the guests. This, indeed, Charles took down, and as the first stage in his rebuilding, commissioned Inigo Jones to erect a permanent hall in stone. It was duly completed – the first Palladian building in England – and its ceiling superbly painted by Rubens, on the theme of 'The Apotheosis of James I'. Like many other fine

English state buildings, it has undergone neglect and vicissitudes, but it has now been faithfully restored, and is used for state banquets again. The plans for the rest of Charles's projected palace survive. But he lacked the money to carry them out, and the Civil War brought all his building operations to a stop. Even the expenditure on the Banqueting House was resented, and parliament expressed its feelings by executing Charles in front of it.

The Civil War changed the whole atmosphere of Whitehall. Tilting was never resumed, and the Yard, tennis-courts and cockpit were cleared away to make an exercise-ground, now Horse Guards Parade. But there were still deer, cows and goats in St James's Park, as we can tell from a fine painting showing Charles II walking on the spot where Downing Street now stands. He lived at Whitehall, where his bedroom led into the apartments of his trusted secretary, Will Chiffinch, known as 'Master of the Backstairs', a secret exit on to the river, which the King used for

Below A German print of Charles I's execution. 'The expenditure on the Banqueting House was resented and Parliament expressed its feelings by executing Charles in front of it.'

65

Overleaf Charles II walking in Horse Guards Parade with Whitehall in the background.

nocturnal excursions. Charles, like his father, had a plan to
rebuild the palace, and in his last year Wren set up a range of
buildings at right-angles to the Banqueting House. But this
scheme, too, lapsed for lack of money; and in the 1690s, two
disastrous fires left the palace a gutted ruin. Royalty now left
Whitehall for good, moving to St James's and Kensington.

This departure both reflected and symbolized the growing
divorce between the monarch, on the one hand, and the operations of his government. Once the officers of state had lived in the
royal palaces, and travelled round with their master. Even in
Charles II's day, his house was still an active centre of administration, though the major departments, such as the Treasury,
Exchequer and Chancery, had long since acquired their separate
headquarters. The great wars against Louis XIV led to a vast
expansion in the activities and personnel of government, and the
dominance of parliament in the constitution increased the
tendency of the state offices to settle in its neighbourhood. Thus
modern Whitehall came into existence, no longer royal, but very
much the official quarter. The Horse Guards, the headquarters of
the army administration, went up in 1663–4, the first public
office to be purpose-built; the Admiralty, next door, followed
three decades later. These buildings, and others, had to be
constantly altered and enlarged as the work of government
grew. There was no point at which they could be successfully
fused into a unitary scheme. This has its drawbacks: government
Whitehall had, and has, a ragged appearance, as did royal
Whitehall before it. But it has many compensations: architectural felicities which make little sense in conjunction, but are
delightful in themselves. Thus, there is the pillared screen added
to the Admiralty building by Robert Adam in the 1750s, one of
his earliest and most successful conceits. Or the façade of the Old
Treasury (now the Cabinet Offices) by William Kent. Or Dover
House (the Scottish Office) by Henry Holland, perhaps the most
elegant building in Whitehall. Often the remodelling incorporated old features, so that the later façades conceal, as it were,
archaeological layers of the old. The panelling in the great Board
Room at the Admiralty was taken from the earlier building, and
the magnificent carving of the fireplace, incorporating Oughtred's
Ring Dial and Gunter's Quadrant – and framing a wind-compass
by Robert Norden – is almost certainly the work of Grinling
Gibbons. British ministers and civil servants worked, and to a
great extent still work, in a medley of styles from different epochs,
which suggest both the muddle and the continuity of British
constitutional history, and act as a reminder that – the Civil War
apart – there has been no great convulsion in our past.

The Civil Service itself emerged in the same haphazard
fashion. Until the mid-seventeenth-century, great officials conducted state business largely from their own households. Lord
Burghley, Queen Elizabeth's leading minister for forty years,
made no distinction between his personal secretaries and those of

his officials who were employed by the Crown, both groups forming part of his establishment, and usually living under his roof. Private and official papers (and often financial accounts) were inextricably mixed, so that when Burghley's colleague, the great foreign minister Sir Francis Walsingham, died, the government simply seized all of his papers (most of which were then lost). Burghley was luckier, for he had sons to defend his property, and his vast collection of state and private documents are preserved at Hatfield House. The Chancery and the Exchequer had always kept its documents (the Exchequer pipe-rolls run continuously from 1154 until the system was changed in 1832), but the concept of government files was a late-seventeenth-century invention, and state papers were treated as private property. The personal element in the Civil Service survived much longer. When Sir Robert Walpole got his hands on the levers of power, he carefully filled every post in the offices he controlled, down to the doorkeepers and footmen, with his political supporters, or their relatives and dependents. He usually had to wait until death removed the incumbent: for most government posts were not subject to retirement or dismissal, except in the gravest circumstances, and were in effect held as life-freeholds, like the benefices of Anglican clergymen. Thus, in the 1800s, a King's Messenger was discovered to have opened dispatches and used the information he gleaned to speculate in the Funds; after a cabinet meeting it was decided to take the grave step of dismissing him, since it was discovered there was no statute under which he could be prosecuted!

Each department, in the eighteenth century, was fiercely independent, with its own accountancy procedures. Indeed, its own funds were often supplied, not by the Treasury, but by a direct lien on specific forms of revenue. The system was immensely complex, and corrupt: ministers like Walpole used public money, in enormous quantities, to finance private trading-ventures, and lesser men abused their trust in proportion. But each aspect of it was time-hallowed, and when Lord Shelburne began to centralize it in the 1770s, he was bitterly assailed. The beneficiaries of the system called him 'the Jesuit of Berkeley Square' (where he lived), after the Portuguese *eminence grise*, Father Malagrida; and this occasioned one of Oliver Goldsmith's notorious lapses in tact, when he said to Shelburne: 'I never could understand why they called you after Malagrida, for I hear he was a good sort of fellow.' Shelburne's reforms were continued and completed by his brightest pupil, William Pitt the Younger. They made the Treasury the sole office empowered to receive and disburse public funds, and so made its approval for estimates essential; the effect was to establish 'Treasury Control' – a concept still maintained today – over all other departments, and to make the Treasury the power centre of Whitehall. In the process, corruption became virtually impossible, and a great many sinecure offices were abolished. Such a simple and efficient system may seem obvious to

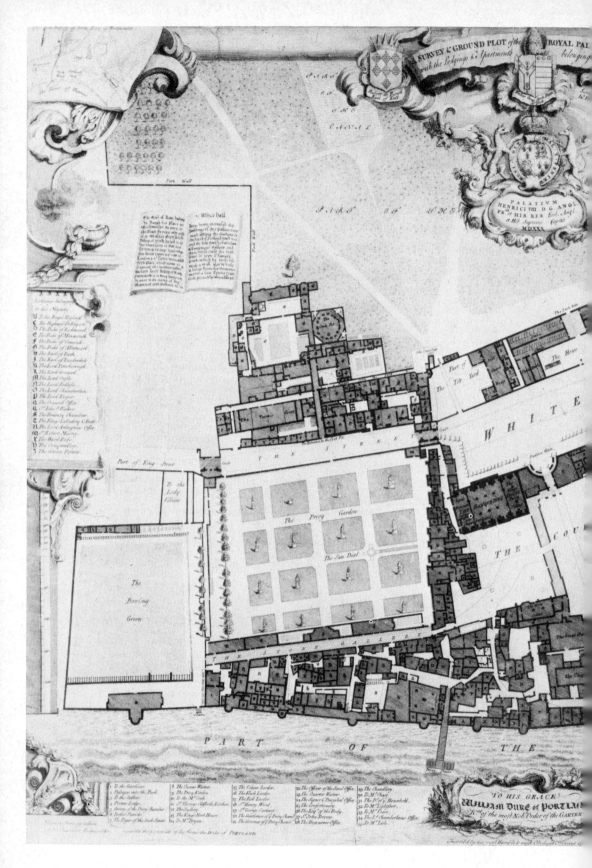

Groundplan of Whitehall, 1680, showing the complexity of buildings, royal apartments, government offices, ministers' residences, parks, gardens, and areas of recreation.

us; but it had hitherto eluded mankind. Since then, all states
have adopted it, at least in theory.

The methods by which civil servants were recruited was re-
formed much more slowly. Until the mid-nineteenth century,
nomination by ministers, MPs or other influential persons was
the normal channel. A gentlemanly appearance and behaviour
and good handwriting were considered all that was necessary
by way of qualifications, though the novelist Anthony Trollope,
who got a clerkship in the Post Office through a powerful friend
of his mother's, relates that no one even troubled to look at the
handwriting specimen he submitted. The Whitehall Civil Service
was a small world: the census of 1851 revealed that only 1,628
officials manned the central departments of civil government. The
British ruling class felt it was natural that senior civil servants
should be friends, dependents, relatives or nominees of the
ministers whose policies they were charged with carrying out.
And such men were 'obedient servants' in the true sense of the
phrase. With very rare exceptions, they played little part in
shaping policy; most of them were called 'clerks', and clerks they
were, spending their time copying and circulating documents.
'Bureaucratic influence' was a term of abuse, with sinister
Continental overtones. Asked by the young Queen Victoria to
explain what it meant, Lord Palmerston replied:

> In England, the Ministers who are at the head of the several depart-
> ments of the State, are liable any day and every day to defend themselves
> in Parliament, and in order to do this, they must be minutely acquainted
> with all the details of the business of their offices, and the only way of
> being constantly armed with such information is to conduct and direct
> those details themselves.

His under-secretary for many years, Sir George Shee, affirmed
in 1832 that this was exactly what Palmerston did: 'Lord
Palmerston, you know, never consults an under-secretary. He
merely sends out questions to be answered or papers to be
copied . . . our only business is to obtain from the clerks the
information that is wanted.' Palmerston's treatment of his Foreign
Office staff was notoriously harsh. He cut down their coal and
candles, extended their hours, made them work on Sunday, and
expected them to sleep on the premises to fit in with his nocturnal
habits of work. The clerks' room was called 'The Nursery', and
from it they ogled the pretty girls who worked in a dressmaker's
establishment in Fludyer Street, at the back of the Foreign
Office. The owner complained to Palmerston that his officials were
flashing mirrors at the girls, and he dictated an angry minute,
commanding them 'to desist from casting reflections on the young
ladies opposite'. When Palmerston was sacked in 1851, the clerks
were so delighted they illuminated the top storeys of the Foreign
Office with their much-grudged candles.

But the 'gentleman's' Civil Service was ultimately doomed
when the 1832 Reform Bill opened political power to the middle-

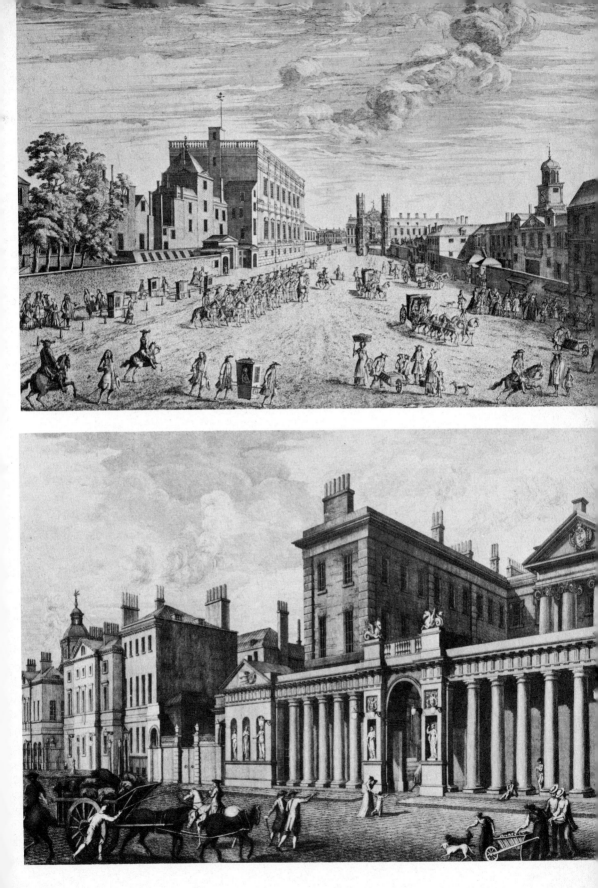

Lord Palmerston, whose strict regime at the Foreign Office typified the authority of ministers over the Civil Service.

classes; it was only a matter of time before they took over the Civil Service, which in any event was expanding to meet the administrative needs of the Age of Reform. Obviously, the aristocratic principle of selection could no longer work. It had to be replaced by selection by merit, that is, competitive examination. British rule in India had already shown the way: running a sub-continent of a hundred million people demanded a professional administrative class, and competition was used to recruit it. The system had produced geniuses like Macaulay, Grote and James Mill, and seemed to have justified itself by results; in 1853 it was extended to all Indian posts. These lessons were applied to Britain. Selection by exam was recommended by the Northcote–Trevelyan Report, and two years later in 1855, the Civil Service Commission was set up to implement it.

In the second half of the nineteenth century, selection by merit seemed to many to embody Darwin's principle of the survival of the fittest: senior civil servants ceased to regard themselves as fortunate gentlemen who had got cushy jobs by influence, and took on the role of mandarins, men who had risen to the top by sheer brain-power – the élite. Thus they arrogated to themselves an increasing share in the shaping of policy, and learned to exercise that 'bureaucratic influence' the opponents of reform had deplored. So long as Gladstone, a man brought up on Palmerstonian principles of ministerial control of detail, remained in power, the Treasury resisted the mandarin take-over. After his departure, civil servants moved swiftly into the vacuum: the age of the all-powerful 'Treasury Knights' was dawning, and the result was a progressive decline of parliamentary and ministerial control of central financial and economic policy.

At the Foreign Office, the change can be dated almost precisely, to the early months of 1906. In January, the long-time permanent head of the Foreign Office, Sir Thomas Sanderson, retired. He had been appointed by the old system of parliamentary nomination, had served Palmerston as private secretary for many years, and was thoroughly imbued with the old tradition that ministers gave orders, and civil servants obeyed them. He was not above copying dispatches himself, when business pressed, and his chief anxiety was to keep the 'clerks' up to sartorial scratch by obliging them to wear tall hats in the Season. When he left, the mandarins took over, under a weak and inexperienced minister, Sir Edward Grey, who had never even visited the Continent. The system of files was changed to allow officials to minute advice before dispatches reached the Foreign Secretary; senior men were relieved of routine duties to give them time to ponder foreign policy and write lengthy memoranda, which were circulated to the cabinet – the age of the 'think tank' was dawning, too.

The mandarin upsurge was marked by an increasing tendency to keep the more arcane secrets of foreign policy from the eyes of parliament, or even of the cabinet. Thus the extension of the Entente Cordiale with France into a military alliance aimed against Germany – marked by secret staff-talks which were pushed by the Foreign Office – was hidden from the cabinet until it acquired irresistible momentum, and was never debated in parliament at all. The process whereby Britain drifted into the Armageddon of 1914 took place outside the system of constitutional and democratic control. It was masterminded by Sir Eyre Crowe, a zealous proponent of the mandarin caste, known to his colleagues as 'The Bird'. He called politicians 'interfering busybodies' and had such a passion for secrecy that only one photograph of himself is known to exist: it hangs in the Permanent Under-secretary's room at the Foreign Office.

The rise of the professional and all-powerful civil servant was marked by a vast building programme in Whitehall. Once again, the scheme as a whole was never carried through to completion; but enough was done to give Whitehall a predominantly Victorian appearance. The design of the new Foreign Office was entrusted to Sir George Gilbert Scott, and he produced a plan which Palmerston dismissed as 'a hideous Gothic structure', 'frightful' and 'like a Continental cathedral' (it was later used for St Pancras Station). Sent back to his drawing-board by Palmerston with orders to create an Italianate design, Scott turned in an Italo-Byzantine mish-mash, which the Prime Minister likewise rejected, and the neo-Florentine edifice which now stands can fairly be regarded as a Palmerstonian creation. It is now very much in aesthetic favour, and a recent plan to replace it by a glass-and-concrete box was heavily defeated by public sentiment. The adjoining India Office (now part of the FO in the Foreign and Commonwealth Office) is in some ways even more impressive: its great courtyard radiates the subtle blend of English and Oriental which made the Indian Empire unique, though it is disfigured by a hideous collection of pre-fabs at its base – a modern instance of the way in which 'temporary' buildings have always formed part of the Whitehall landscape. Below the Foreign Office, the late Victorians set up the combined Treasury and Home Office, which might be described as a Victorian adaptation of English Baroque: with its domed towers and circular courtyard, it has a deliberate flavour of Wren, and thus serves as a reminder – albeit a debased one – of the magnificent seventeenth-century Whitehall Palace that was never built.

These massive nineteenth-century buildings were not the work of geniuses; but they are carefully-planned artifacts, made with consummate workmanship, and adorned with a wealth of decorative detail which modern methods of stone-cleaning have brilliantly revealed. They are already encrusted with history. From the majestic office of the Foreign Secretary, on the evening of 3 August 1914, Sir Edward Grey gazed sadly over St James's Park as the gaslamps were extinguished one by one: 'The lamps are going out all over Europe,' he said. 'We shall not see them lit again in our lifetime.'

Edward Grey – his weakness
confirmed the rise of the
Foreign Office 'mandarins'
and the consequent lessening
of ministerial authority.

In a sense he was right: Whitehall, at least, was never to be
quite the same again. The Great War saw the expansion of
government on a truly modern scale, and Whitehall lost its
monopoly of the physical machine. During the last sixty years,
government departments have spread all over London, indeed
all over the provinces; there is a constant urge to 'decentralize',
and at one time there was even wild talk of transferring
Whitehall itself to York, in a desperate attempt to relieve
London congestion. Yet the twentieth century has changed
the physical appearance of Whitehall remarkably little, considering the momentous revolution in government which has
taken place. There has been some tinkering: in 1960 the Cabinet
Offices, except for the façade, were gutted and rebuilt. The
Cenotaph marks the point where the old 'Street' ended: designed
by Edward Lutyens, on the inspiration of the Parthenon, it is
deceptively subtle, for all its apparent vertical and horizontal
lines are, in fact, convex; and it, too, is coming back into aesthetic

Office of the Cabinet
Secretary in the old Treasury
building, Whitehall.

fashion. The only major addition is the Ministry of Defence, or
'Quadragon', and this can scarcely be called modern: it was
designed by Vincent Harris as long ago as 1913, before the lights
went out; but work began only in 1945 and it was not completed
until 1959. Sir Nicholas Pevsner has dismissed it as 'a monument
of tiredness'. It is also a monument to the English habit of
incorporating bits of the old with the new: for, embedded in this
bare and unpleasing work of functionalism are not only
Henry VIII's wine-cellar, which now, as Pevsner says, has acquired
a Piranesi grandeur in its new setting, but portions of other ancient
structures, including a Wren terrace. In front, too, is a reminder
of the old Durham House which once rested on this site, in the
shape of a statue of Sir Walter Raleigh. For Sir Walter had
apartments in Durham House, including a study where he wrote
his poems and his projects for conquering the Americas. John
Aubrey described it as 'a little turret that looked into and over the
Thames, and has the prospect which is as pleasant perhaps as
any in the World, and which not only refreshes the eie-sight but
cheers the spirits, and (to speake my mind) I believe enlarges an
ingeniose man's thoughts'. Apart from Sir Walter, the only
politician whose statue mounts guard over Whitehall is the Eighth

Duke of Devonshire, 'Harty-Tarty': the rest are imperial warriors: the Duke of Cambridge, Haig, Wolseley, Roberts, Kitchener and Clive. Notable civil servants like Crowe or Sir Warren Fisher, who dominated the Treasury and Whitehall in the inter-war years, have left no visible monuments to their power. But their legacy is fiercely defended from behind stone walls, which conceal it from prying public eyes.

Whitehall has never been the exclusive domain of either royalty or government. There were tenements here as long as history records, and Dickens describes humble beer-shops, patronized by Thames bargees, along the Whitehall waterfront. Even today, there is a raffish theatre, a pub or two, and private apartments – many of them due to be swept away when Parliament, for the first time, crosses Westminster Bridge Road and invades Whitehall territory. It seems against all probability, looking back on its long history, that Whitehall will be allowed to keep its present shape. Soon the itch to rebuild will re-assert itself. Monumental plans will take shape; but, if precedent is any guide, they too will never be completed, and new Whitehalls will retain fragments and essences of the old.

5 ST BARTHOLOMEW'S HOSPITAL

From Alms to Welfare

The hospital and its surroundings – 'like a major Cambridge college of the Augustan era'.

EXTERNALLY, St Bartholomew's, or Bart's, as it is known throughout the medical world, looks like a major Cambridge college of the Augustan era: separate stone-faced classical blocks, forming three sides of a square (the fourth is now made up by a 1930s addition), with a dominant gateway conceived in the reign of Queen Anne, but wholly reconstructed shortly before the accession of Queen Victoria. In fact, Bart's is a characteristic English institution: an instrument of modern medical therapy and research – and perhaps the most famous teaching hospital in the West – housed behind an eighteenth-century façade, but tracing its origins and ethos back to the early Middle Ages. As such, it epitomizes a great deal of English medical history.

Until very recently, hospitals were designed exclusively for the poor. They were charitable institutions, endowed by the rich to keep out of circulation those whom life and nature had defeated: the destitute, the insane, the orphans, the geriatrics, the incorrigible, the infectious and the incurable. The first such recorded was an isolation hospital, set up on an island in the Tiber after a fierce outbreak of plague in Rome in 293 BC. It was later rechristened St Bartholomew's, after the mysterious, perhaps mythical, apostle who converted Armenia, was flayed alive for his pains, and whose symbol became the butcher's knife. Flourishing towns did not want the sick, or the dead, within their walls: it was too dangerous. West Smithfield, outside the London perimeter, had been a burial-ground since Roman times. Such cemeteries surrounded the City walls, as did small buildings where lepers, and the sick poor, were dumped, to be cared for by lowly churchmen.

The early twelfth century was a time of economic and intellectual expansion. New scientific ideas were being transmitted to the West from the Arabs, via the crusaders who had penetrated the Near East. In particular, the crusaders had set up purpose-built hospitals, manned by specialist groups of knights, to cure their warriors. Possibly their influence inspired Rahere, one of Henry I's court, to set up a new hospital at Smithfield, in 1123, to replace

Overleaf *Henry VIII Granting the Charter to the Barber-Surgeons* by Holbein.

The Martyrdom of T.Loseby, H.Ramsey, T.Thirtell, Margt. Hide & Agnes Stanley in Smithfield.

Five Protestant victims of Queen Mary's persecution. Over two hundred were burned as heretics at Smithfield in her reign.

the ramshackle hovels which housed the sick outside this part of London. Tradition calls Rahere a 'jester', though the sixteenth-century London antiquary, John Stow, is doubtless more accurate in describing him as 'a pleasant-witted gentleman, and therefore in his time called the King's minstrel'. He was certainly rich: the story goes that he decided to turn from worldly pleasures after recovering from a desperate illness – hence his dedication to St Bartholomew. For his foundation he chose the Regular Canons of St Augustine, a relatively new foundation, and an aristocratic one. The canons lived communally, but not subject to the restrictions imposed on most orders: Chaucer's famous sporting monk was an Augustinian. Rahere may merely have wanted a comfortable billet for his old age, for his foundation (which, of course, was tax free) consisted of the hospital and a much larger priory, of which he became the first prior. Their relative importance can be judged by their annual incomes at the Dissolution of the Monasteries, which, Stow records, were £35 and £653 respectively. Moreover, Rahere secured from the King, ten years after the foundation, the valuable perquisite of holding an annual fair on 24 August, the saint's feast-day. Bartholomew's Fair stretched to a fortnight, became the greatest gathering of cloth-merchants in the kingdom, and an annual summer carnival for Londoners until tidy-minded Victorians abolished it in 1855.

West Smithfield can scarcely have been chosen for its salubri-ousness. It was flat: 'Smoothfield' was its original name, and the Fleet River, bounding it on the west, overflowed into marshes. Part of it was a horse-pond, the biggest just outside London, and the availability of water made it the concentration-point for London's chief live-cattle market; cattle were bought, sold and killed there until the mid-nineteenth century, when the slaughter-house was transferred to Islington. The place was also a dump for City sewage and rubbish. In one corner were the Elms, vast trees used for the hanging and dismembering of common criminals. Later the trees were chopped down to supply fuel for the burning of heretics, who had bags of gunpowder strapped between their legs if wind, rain, or damp wood threatened a prolonged agony. Over five hundred were burnt alive at Smithfield, more than two hundred of them in three brief years of Bloody Mary's reign. The Field was also a place for tournaments – Alice Perrers, Edward III's notorious mistress, rode there from Cheapside, dressed as the Lady of the Sun, for the last jousts of the reign – and an assembly-ground for rebellious peasants, swarming from the provinces to threaten the government. There, William Walworth, the fish-monger-mayor of London, mortally wounded Wat Tyler in 1381. Tyler was dragged to Bart's to be tidied up, before being hanged on the Elms. The bellowing of cattle, the screams of criminals and heresiarchs, the noise of battle, tumult, bargaining and holiday, heat, dust and countless flies in summer, intolerable mud in winter – above all, the stench of decaying livestock and humanity: these have formed the inescapable environment of Bart's patients throughout most of its history. The Medieval mind accepted this incongruity without question: life, warfare, business, ill-health, madness, punishment and death all reflected the mysterious workings of God's providence, which were to be seen as a whole, not isolated and tidied away into separate compart-ments.

In any case, there was little the hospital could do for its inmates, who came there to die. Rejected by their families, they probably thought themselves fortunate to leave the world in relative dignity, and with the comforts of the church. When Edward III confirmed Bart's charter, the establishment provided for a master and eight assistants, plus four sisters, 'to see the poor served'. No mention of physicians and surgeons. Not that they would have been of much use. Medieval medicine was imprisoned in the teachings of Galen, the personal physician to Marcus Aurelius, whose encyclopaedic writings remained not merely the conventional wisdom, but enforced dogma, for over a millennium.

Above Roger Bacon, the thirteenth-century scientist whose empirical methods were well ahead of the dogmatic suppositions of his contemporaries.

Galen had used drugs, and may have been a skilful diagnostician, but his basic concept that the body was a mere vehicle for the soul, and so governed by humours, elements and the stars, with treatment to be determined by their interaction – all this compounded by a faulty knowledge of anatomy – ruled out empirical trial-and-error methods. His dogmatism made him peculiarly acceptable to a church which was itself dogmatic, and which supervised medicine, so that the effect of Galen's teaching was not merely to discourage experiment but to penalize it. Thus a great English empirical scientist like Roger Bacon (1214–94) could not get his work published until long after his death, and even his lectures brought him fourteen years in episcopal prisons. Most physicians diagnosed and prescribed by a combination of looking at the heavens and inspecting the patient's urine while taking his pulse. Chemistry, or alchemy, had as its object the discovery of elixirs, and anatomy was not advanced by the dissection of animals, all that the church would allow.

There were some good doctors in the Middle Ages, many trained at the University of Montpellier. One such was the Englishman John of Gaddesden (1280–1361) who doubtless visited the wards at Bart's, already the most convenient centre for English doctors to acquire clinical experience (though another major hospital, St Thomas's, had been founded in 1215). He had served in Edward III's wars, and been present at Crecy; in the fourteenth century, as at most other periods, war was the great engine of medical advance. In his one surviving work, *A Treatise on the Fistula,* he lays down general rules for the conduct of surgeons, which are both sensible and characteristic of his profession. The qualities required were tact, taciturnity, sobriety and much study and observation. Anticipating the rules of the modern General Medical Council, he insists: 'A surgeon should not look too boldly at the lady or daughter or other fair women in great men's houses, nor offer to kiss them, or touch them openly or secretly.' He must 'boldly adjust his fee to the patient's status in life', and should on no account 'ask too little, for this is bad both for the market and the patient'. Chaucer used John as his model for his 'Doctor of Physick':

> Well could he guess the ascending of the star,
> Wherein his patient's fortunes settled were,
> He knew the course of every malady,
> Where it of cold, or hot, or moist, or dry,
> And where they engendred, and of what humour,
> He was a very parfit practisour.

'Parfit' by the standards of the day; John was evidently a traditionalist, if an accomplished one.

Medieval medicine was eroded by the Renaissance. The Basel doctor, Paracelsus (1493–1541), openly denounced Galen as nonsense and dogmatism as the enemy of progress. He angered the authorities and his colleagues, but he made many cures: 'I

Opposite Medical progress: an anatomy lesson, 1581.

415 REAL. COL. CREM.   DE VISCER. LIB. XI. 416

Intestina à ventricu-
lo exoriuntur, eademq́
pene substantia viden-
tur licet aliquantulu
tenuiore. Situs eorū
est, ab inferiori ven-
triculi orificio ad Anū
vsque, abdominisq́ ma-
iorem parte occupant.
Veteres Anatomici in-
testina in sex partes
distinxere, distinctísq́
singulas nominibus

appellauere. Ego vero
si post tot seculorū re-
cepta vocabula noui
aliquid in mediū pro-
ferre fas esset, int=stina
duo esse dicerem quorū
alterū tenue est, crassū
alterū. Sed vt aliorum
vestigia sequamur, sex
esse dicemus intestina,
duodenū, ieiunū, ileon, cæ-
cum, colan, rectūmque

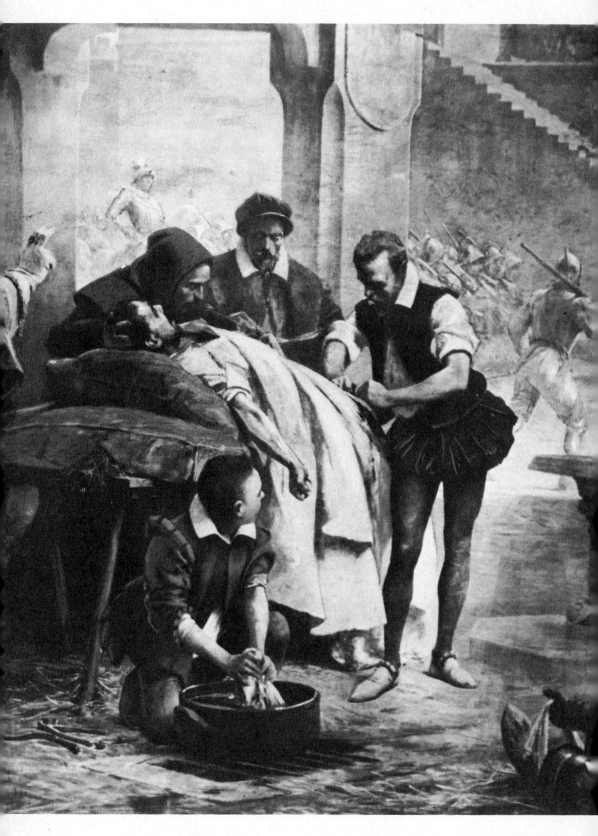

Above Richard Wiseman, the first notable English surgeon.

pleased no one except the sick whom I healed,' he boasted. On a more scientific basis, Andreas Vesalius (1514–64), the Flemish physician to Charles v, demolished Galen's anatomy by stealing a criminal's skeleton from the gallows, and later dissecting human corpses. His findings, published in 1543 and superbly illustrated by a pupil of Titian, began to teach the medical world the true structure and functioning of the body, and such novelties were publicized in England by the new Royal College of Physicians incorporated in 1551.

English medicine was beginning to organize itself, and Bart's played the leading role in the process. With the dissolution of the church foundations in the 1540s, Crown and City cooperated to reorganize the welfare element the church had provided. Henry VIII re-founded Bart's as a secular establishment, which is why his statue adorns the gateway. Almost on his deathbed he came to a deal with the City authorities, carried through by his son, Edward VI, under which a system of royal hospitals was established for London, and with a massive injection of City funds to bolster the old monastic sources of revenue: Bart's for the sick, St Thomas's for the permanently infirm, Christ's for the support and education of poor children, Bridewell for vagabonds and unemployed, and Mary of Bethlehem (Bedlam) for the insane. This had the merit of a rational structure, though its capacity was soon overtaken by the vast expansion of London. It had the further merit of concentrating medical therapy in Bart's. Not that Tudor medicine was impressive. That wise woman, Elizabeth I, who had seen her young half-brother in effect murdered by his physicians, disliked physic of almost any kind, especially the potions of tinctured mercury, gold and silver proffered to the rich. She forbade her great servant, Lord Burghley, to take them, and sent herbal remedies of her own; both lived to serene old age.

Indeed, even the post-Galen medical profession proved an obstacle to progress. The physicians were supreme, empowered by statute to license all practitioners in London and within a seven-mile radius (bishops issued licences for the rest of the country), insisting on Oxbridge degrees for their members, and Latin as the sole medium of communication. They wore gloves and an enveloping robe, with a 'nose bag' consisting of an impregnated sponge to guard against infection (this later took the form of a cane, with a perforated gold top, which the physician waved in front of him). Often they refused to come close to the patient, and prescribed from chairs. They could perform surgery, but the lowlier barber-surgeons could not administer physic, and the still more humble apothecaries and midwives, who often possessed more valuable experience, were even more severely circumscribed. The physician was described in 1602 as 'a great commander, who had as subordinate to him the cooks for diet, the surgeons for manual operation, the apothecaries for confecting and preparing medicines'.

But kings could break their own rules, and did. The 'father of

Left Ambrose Paré, 'father of modern surgery', at work during the siege of Metz.

EXERCITATIO
ANATOMICA DI
MOTV CORDIS ET SAN
GVINIS IN ANIMALI-
BVS,

GVILIELMI HARVEI ANGL

*Medici Regii, & Profeſſoris Anatomiæ in Col-
legio Medicorum Londinenſi.*

FRANCOFVRTI,
Sumptibus **GVILIELMI FITZERI.**
ANNO M. DC. XXVIII.

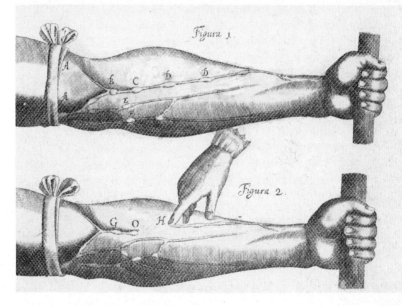

modern surgery', the great Frenchman Ambrose Paré (1510–90),
was a despised barber-surgeon, who knew no Latin or Greek, and
trusted to observation rather than books, but who nevertheless
served four grateful French monarchs. 'I dressed him, God
healed him', recurs throughout his memoirs – an observation
with which the best doctors agreed until the age of antibiotics.
He got his experience working in the wards of the Paris Hôtel-
Dieu, the French equivalent of Bart's; and in England it was to
Bart's that doctors turned increasingly to learn, the poor class
providing the guinea-pigs.

Medical progress was inseparable from war, and politics. The dominance of the conservative physicians, who treated 'empiric' as a synonym for 'unlicensed practitioner' (they had the power to prosecute both), and who were closely linked to the High Church universities and the court, aroused opposition from innovators and political radicals alike. They think, wrote the Elizabethan surgeon John Hall, 'that only to physic belongeth theory and speculation, and that to surgery belongeth only practice . . . [whereas if] theory and practice go not together, whether ye call it physic or surgery, I dare boldly affirm that there is in them no manner of perfection worthy of commendation.' Intellectuals, led by Francis Bacon, moved strongly in favour of experimentation in all sciences, and the downfall of the Stuart tyranny in 1640, with the lifting of restrictions on printing, brought a flood of empirical works from the presses. In the Civil War, the physicians sided broadly with the King, the barber-surgeons with Parliament; the apothecaries were still more radical. There were exceptions. The first notable English surgeon, Richard Wiseman (1622–76) fought for Charles, as did Bacon's doctor, William Harvey (1578–1657), though the latter was careful to get Parliament's permission. But it was noted by observers that among 'the great advantages the parliament hath of His Majesty' was the much greater choice 'both of land- and sea-surgeons', with a corresponding effect on casualties. Among the Parliamentarians was the first great English clinical physician, Thomas Sydenham (1624–89), who commanded a troop of Cromwell's horse. 'Anatomy, botany, nonsense! No, young man, go to the bedside, there alone you can learn disease' – this was his advice to Hans Sloane, later Queen Anne's doctor.

Thus empiricism triumphed in the test of war; nor could the clock be put back entirely by the Restoration. Harvey, physician to Bart's, had lectured on the circulation of the blood, probably the most important discovery in the history of medicine, as early as 1616, and published his findings (abroad) in 1628. The interregnum hastened the acceptance of his work, and the formation of a body of learned men in 1645 – soon to blossom into the Royal Society – established the supremacy of experimental science, rapidly confirmed by the Newtonian revolution in physics. Medical men were now aware they had to look for rules, for cause and effect, and confirm them by observation, experiment and case-books: they turned increasingly to the big hospitals, above all to Bart's where they combined free attendance in the wards with lucrative private practice. The hospitals themselves were reorganized, and rebuilt on a grander scale: Bedlam in 1675–6, followed by Thomas's; then Guy's in 1721–5, and Bart's in 1730–59. The architect of Bart's was James Gibbs, the gifted Aberdonian who designed Oxford's Radcliffe Camera and Cambridge's Senate House. The result was elegant, the first London building for which Bath stone was used, and practical: big, open-plan wards, heated by fires fed from the Royal Windsor forest: and the staircase was adorned by two large Hogarths (he was a Governor), *The Pool of Bethesda* and *The Good Samaritan*.

These eighteenth-century hospitals were mirrors of their time. As in prisons, patients who could afford to tip got better beds and more attentive treatment. Offices were held as freeholds, subject neither to dismissal nor pensions. There were customs, ceremonials and perks peculiar to each. At Bedlam, the public was admitted on Sunday, on payment of a penny (later raised to twopence) to watch the antics of the lunatics. It was one of the wonders of London, a must for foreign visitors; and those who ran it argued that the company of the sane, conversation and laughter invigorated the inmates and helped their condition. The mad, it was claimed, should not be hidden away from the world (as they are today, sometimes in conditions little better than Bedlam). Thus the spirit of open acceptance of calamity, so characteristic of the ancient and Medieval world, lingered on. But it was eroded by the growing sensitivity of the late-eighteenth century. After Hogarth published his enormously successful print of his Bedlam canvas, the last in his *Rake's Progress*, the movement to separate the suffering from the public got under way. Bedlam was first, in 1770, restricted to well-dressed ticket holders, then to relatives. Bart's and other hospitals were cleared of riff-raff and hangers-on. The age of the strict visiting-hour had dawned.

Of course, controlling visitors, quite apart from reducing the risk of infection, made it easier for doctors to perform effectively in hospitals which were ceasing to be places in which the poor came to die and were, increasingly, short-stay centres where cures could be attempted. Indeed, in the eighteenth and nineteenth centuries the incurable poor were either not admitted at all, or rapidly moved to the workhouse when the efforts of doctors failed. The extent to which workhouses were used as buildings where the sick were 'stored' was not realized until national statistics began to become available in the mid-Victorian period. Louisa Twining, the great workhouse reformer, found that in 1851 there were less than 8,000 beds in public hospitals throughout England and Wales; by 1871, there were still only about 20,000. Bart's had 675 beds, serving 150,000 people annually, plus a 75-bed convalescent home in Kent; and it taught 400 students. Meanwhile, some 50,000 of the 157,740 indoor paupers in 1869 were, in fact, hospital cases: the workhouses, said Miss Twining, were 'hospitals for those who are incurable'. Not until London, in the late 1860s, began to build 'infirmaries' (gradually renamed hospitals in the period 1931–48), was any effort made to tackle the basic problem of indigent illness.

The contribution made by hospitals like Bart's depended on three factors: the training and skill of individual doctors, the progress of medical science, and the organization of, and social attitudes to, medical care. The first depended very much on

Overleaf left The Banqueting Hall: the only remaining ceiling painted by Rubens. It shows the *Apotheosis of James I*.

Overleaf right Two views of Berkeley Castle, built to keep the multitudes in subjection.

personality, and the great London hospitals have always prided themselves on producing 'characters'. Some were prodigiously hard-working, like William Smellie (1697–1763), the first real obstetric specialist, who attended 1,150 cases of labour in London, and trained 900 students; or like John Coakley Lettsom (1744–1815), who wore out three pairs of carriage-horses a day while visiting, and attended 82,000 patients in the year 1795 alone. Of him it was said:

> When any sick to me apply,
> I physics, bleeds and sweats 'em.
> If, after that, they choose to die,
> What's that to me? – I Lettsom.

Above William Smellie, the first specialist in obstetrics.

Some doctors, like Edward Jenner (1749–1823), the first to introduce vaccination, preferred a country practice: Jenner worked in Berkeley, Gloucestershire, where his father had been Vicar, throughout a very busy life. But the great majority radiated from the London wards, where their eccentricities became folklore. There was John Radcliffe, the famous Oxford infirmarian (1650–1714), and physician to William III and Mary, who pioneered the curt tradition. He told his even more famous pupil, Richard Mead (1673–1754): 'I love you Mead, and I'll give you an infallible recipe for success in practice: use all mankind ill.' John Abernathy (1764–1831), chief surgeon at Bart's for a generation, believed all diseases not surgical or external were the result of digestive factors, and his favourite remedies were calomel and the blue pill; rich hypochondriacs he sent to a fictitious Dr Robertson in Inverness, believing that the frustration of the journey (it took a week) would turn their minds to other things.

Above Edward Jenner, who introduced the practice of vaccination.

Physicians relied heavily on bleeding by leeches, bred at Bart's in a vast aquatic tank; but the surgeons, at least, worked hard. Before anaesthetics, speed was essential lest the patient die of shock. William Cheselden of Thomas's (1688–1752) could extract a stone, the commonest operation, in a minute or less – his record was fifty-four seconds – and he reduced the mortality rate to seventeen per cent. With amputations, the rate was twenty-five per cent or more. Surgeons operated in cast-off coats, and physical strength was a key factor. At the news of the Battle of Waterloo, Sir Charles Bell (1744–1842), the great nerve specialist, went there immediately, and operated until his 'clothes were stiff with blood' and his arms 'powerless with the exertion of using the knife'. Robert Liston (1794–1847) went on the record as the fastest surgeon in history, with a bunch of silk ligatures in his buttonhole for convenience: he achieved fame by successfully removing a tumour of the scrotum weighing no less than 44 lb!

It was Liston, in 1846, who first used ether during an operation. Both ether and laughing gas (nitrous oxide) had been identified by Sir Humphry Davy and Michael Faraday a generation before, though they were first used medically in the United States: 'This Yankee dodge,' exclaimed Liston, 'beats mesmerism hollow.'

Anaesthetics allowed surgeons to take their time and perform much more complex tasks: the first real breakthrough in modern medicine. Among the students who watched Liston perform this crucial operation was Joseph Lister (1827–1912). He used the work of Pasteur, in France, on bacteria, to isolate the organic cause of post-operative infection, and so counteract it by employing antiseptics, such as carbolic acid. Lister introduced his new system while operating on a compound fracture in 1865, and it was soon universally adopted: the second great pillar of modern medicine.

The London hospitals were now a forcing-ground of discovery. Sir James Paget (1814–99), leading diagnostician of his age, made his earliest discoveries in his first year as a student at Bart's; as did Thomas Young (1773–1829), the ophthalmologist, whose identification of the effects of the ciliary muscle on the shape of the eye-lens led to his election as a Fellow of the Royal Society, aged twenty-one, while he was still a probationer in the Bart's wards. But Bart's, and other teaching hospitals, could not make their full contribution to medical progress so long as they were regarded with abhorrence by all members of the public who could afford to get their medical treatment (including operations) at home.

One chief problem was nursing. Hospital nurses were drawn from superannuated domestic servants, what one London institution called 'old women of the charwoman class', and were totally untrained. As Florence Nightingale put it, nursing was the work of those 'too weak, too drunken, too dirty, too stolid or too bad to do anything else'. Many were illiterate, signing with a cross for their wages – 6s a week in London, 2s 6d in the provinces. They slept in wooden cages outside the wards, or in ill-ventilated basements, buying and cooking their own food. There was no prospect of promotion, for ward-sisters were drawn from a higher social class: at Bart's, 'widows in reduced circumstances . . . persons who have lived in a respectable rank of life'. The matrons could be classified as ladies, but concerned themselves solely with the administrative task of running the hospital like a big household, and felt no concern for the work of the nurses. Paget said of the Bart's nurses in 1830 that they were 'dull, unobservant and untaught women; of the best it could only be said that they were kindly and careful'. The sisters, he thought, 'had a rough practical knowledge', but it was acquired purely on an experimental basis. In the workhouse-hospitals, the situation was even worse, for virtually the entire nursing staff were elderly ablebodied paupers, paid nothing and taught nothing. Miss Twining found that, in the Strand Workhouse, of eighteen pauper nurses, fourteen were over sixty and four over seventy; only eight could read the labels on the medicine bottles. They were rewarded with gin 'for laying out the dead and other specially repulsive duties'.

Training of nurses had started in England in 1848, before Florence Nightingale's sensationalized work in the Crimea gave

1901 – the operating theatre in Charing Cross Hospital. By this date the richer classes were beginning to go to hospital for treatment, to the great benefit of hospitals generally.

the cause of professional nursing the publicity it needed. But it was her school in St Thomas's, soon copied throughout London and elsewhere, which set the pattern, firmly based as it was on a changing attitude to medical care: 'The purpose of a hospital,' she wrote, 'is to cure the sick rather than act as a storehouse for sick persons.' Otherwise, concentration of the sick was disastrous: cross-infection would kill more than treatment could possibly save – indeed, in her young days 'hospitalitis' was a general term for a whole range of infections.

Miss Nightingale deplored the social stratification of the old nursing profession, and on the whole did not welcome lady-recruits: country-girls, she thought, made the best training-material. But as nursing acquired status, the middle and upper classes invaded it, as, in the Middle Ages, they had invaded the medical profession itself. And lady-entrants, of course, paid for training in the expectation that they would 'occupy the higher situations'. In the long run, this was no bad thing, for the raising of social, as well as professional, standards of nursing helped to

98

win acceptance for hospitalization among the wealthy classes, and so enormously improve the general efficiency and comfort of hospitals. By 1900, the possessing classes were beginning to 'go into hospital' for serious treatment, for the first time in history. Bart's, and others, profited, and found no difficulty in financing new buildings and equipment, and paying their staff reasonable wages. Indeed, there was at one time a real risk that the famous teaching hospitals, while continuing to fulfil their statutory duties to the poor, would be largely taken over as institutions of the rich, as had happened to the Public Schools, which had likewise been founded for the poor at a time when those who could afford it were taught at home. This danger was avoided, partly by the 1930–50 antibiotic revolution, which levelled up treatment in all hospitals; and partly by Aneurin Bevan's National Health Act, and the take-over of the hospitals in 1946–8. Even so, institutions like Bart's, with their special status as teaching-hospitals, form an élite, distinguished by present performance no less than history, riddled with special anomalies and usages.

The story of Bart's shows that medicine, so vital to well-being, and therefore so susceptible to the pressures of private wealth, cannot be separated from the history of its social and political context. Advances in medicine are not simply a matter of putting into practice the latest medical research. In this field, indeed, Bart's is unquestionably one of the world's leading hospitals. It has a number of highly specialized units which are probing the remote frontiers of medical science. Among its elaborate equipment is a machine for pre-diagnosis which can perform twenty separate tests on blood samples at the rate of three hundred an hour. It is developing mechanical means of reducing pre-natal risks in pregnancy, and methods of determining the sex of unborn children. It is enlarging our understanding of that baffling and terrible disease, leukaemia. These are only three examples of how Bart's is sustaining its reputation as a pioneer medical centre. But experience suggests that changes in social attitudes are just as important as increased knowledge in determining the level of public health. The reorganization of Britain's hospital services has integrated Bart's with the London hospital system. Bigger changes may be on the way. For the past century, medical treatment has become increasingly specialized. But there are signs of a movement in the reverse direction, in which sickness and its treatment will be regarded as merely one facet in an interlocking structure of social service – a return, in one sense, to the comprehensiveness of the Medieval approach, planned by a church which taught mankind to see life, and death, as a whole, and of which the original Bart's was a constituent. If this happens, we may be sure that Bart's will both hasten progress, by promoting the work of brilliant individuals, and also, as a corporate entity, act as a powerful restraint on precipitous change – thus fulfilling its tradition as a characteristic English institution.

6 INNER AND MIDDLE TEMPLE

'A Government of Laws, not Men'

'One of the delights of exploring an old town is to pass from a busy street through a low archway, and discover unexpected splendour and tranquillity within': Hare Court in the Temple.

ONE OF THE DELIGHTS of exploring an old town is to pass from a busy street through a low archway, and discover unexpected splendour and tranquillity within. You can find this in Seville and Burgos, in old Moorish cities like Fez and Meknes; most notably, perhaps, in Genoa, where the palaces of the ancient maritime aristocracy make a virtue of concealing their magnificence from the outside world. Such a pleasure was once common in England, now rare. But on the south side of Fleet Street, there is a little gateway, overhung by a half-timbered, early Jacobean house, whose upper storeys jut out into the street. This is Inner Temple Lane, and when you pass through it you enter the innermost sanctum of the English legal profession. Its narrow alleyways and arches, its courts and staircases – marked with the names of forensic luminaries – its lawns and borders descend gradually to the Embankment. Alas, its architectural glories are now diminished; much damage was inflicted by inelegant nineteenth-century 'improvements', and Hitler's Luftwaffe well-nigh demolished the rest, for the post-war buildings which replaced the old ranges are unenterprising and uniform, and even the painstaking restoration of the ruins thought worth saving has left many bitter scars. Yet the atmosphere is still not unlike that of a large Oxbridge college: here, up to a point, is a sense of academic peace, and an awareness of legal quiddities. The two Inns which compose the Temple are self-governing: normal authority stops short at the Fleet Street threshold, and the Benchers of the Inns are allowed to do many things denied to lesser mortals – the law looks after its own. And why should it not? – for in the Temple the structure of the English legal system has been elaborated and defended over many centuries. More than most buildings in England, it can claim to have left its stamp on history. Even the garden itself was the setting for a national tragedy, for there, as Shakespeare relates in *Henry VI, Part I*, Richard Plantagenet and John Beaufort had high words, and plucked the symbols for the future encounters of York and Lancaster, the white rose and the red. As the Earl of Warwick is made to say:

> And here I prophesy: this brawl today,
> Grown to this faction in the Temple garden,
> Shall send between the red rose and the white
> A thousand souls to death and deadly night.

What the brethren of the Inns thought of this aristocratic confrontation on their premises is not recorded; it would not, for sure, be allowed to happen today, for the Benchers take a severe line against rowdyism within their franchise, as minatory notices make clear. Their fifteenth-century predecessors must have been terrified by the imminent prospect of a complete breakdown of the law they were sworn to uphold. Yet in one respect the choice of the Temple as the setting for the first act in a civil war was not inappropriate, for it had become legal territory in the first place only as a result of a monstrous and unpunished state crime, and a grievous flouting of 'due process'.

In the twelfth century, the area covered by the Inns was the property of the Poor Knights of Christ and Solomon's Temple. Their order had been created in the wake of the crusades, to provide a guard for the holy places. They were celibates, not priests, but like other religious organizations they soon acquired property on a prodigious scale. In London, they settled outside the west gate of the City, soon called after them; and within the enclave they built one of their circular churches, on the model of the Temple they guarded. There are four such churches remaining in England (the others, in Cambridge, Northampton and Ludlow Castle, were also once associated with the Templars), but London's, despite war-damage and restorers, is the finest. It was consecrated in 1185 and is a curious blend of pure Norman, and pure early Gothic, nearly sixty feet in diameter, with piers of Purbeck marble, and a thirteenth-century oblong chancel attached. On the floor of the circular nave are the marble effigies of ancient knights: they range from that paladin of early Medieval chivalry, William Marshall, Earl of Pembroke, to Geoffrey de Mandeville, the leading robber-baron of King Stephen's 'anarchy'.

The Templars had many privileges: their church was, and still is, a 'royal peculiar', like Westminster Abbey, exempt from any episcopal jurisdiction. They were also a very mixed bunch – like their knightly effigies. When the loss of Jerusalem deprived them of their original function, they devoted their custodial resources to banking, and became the creditors of kings as well as lesser folk. This was their undoing. In the early fourteenth century, Philip the Fair, the ambitious king of France, turned on the Templars to finance his wars, and persuaded his puppet-pope, Clement V, to arraign the members of the order on a multiplicity of fake charges, ranging from blasphemy and devil-worship to sodomy. Not until Stalin organized his great purge and the Moscow 'trials', was there such a highly-organized and ruthless perversion of justice. In Paris alone thirty-six knights died under torture; most confessed to save their lives; in May 1310 some fifty-four recalci-

According to Shakespeare it was in the Temple Garden that Richard Plantagenet and John Beaufort chose the emblems which gave a name to the Wars of the Roses.

trants were burned to death, and four years later, when the Grand-Master and the Master of Normandy repudiated the confessions on behalf of their order, they were roasted alive. In England, the ecclesiastical authorities protested strongly at the pope's instructions that confessions were to be obtained by similar means; they said that torture was unknown under English law, and that professional torturers did not exist. In the end, it seems, torturers were imported, confessions obtained, and the order broken up – though the knights were comfortably pensioned off, thus adumbrating the procedure Henry VIII followed when he dissolved the monasteries.

In London, the Temple property passed to the Knights Hospitallers of St John, who seemed to have had no use for it. At

LORD CHANCELLOR
HATTON 1589

TANDEM SI

Lord Chancellor Hatton:
'There are now more at the
bar in one house than there
were at all the Inns of Court
when I was a young man.'

all events, they leased off portions of it to professors of Common Law, and their pupils who had come to study in London. Thus the Temple became an Inn of Court, or rather two Inns, for though there is no obvious visible distinction between the Inner and Middle Temple, even today, their separation dates from very early days, and is jealously maintained on both sides. Other legal Inns were growing up in London, as the central royal courts became more wide-ranging and more cases were brought to them. North of Fleet Street was Lincoln's Inn; to the east of it, Gray's Inn; and scattered about the western fringes of the City and its suburbs were nine Inns of Chancery, which taught the Continental-style equity law practised in the Lord Chancellor's court. Lincoln's, Gray's and the two Temple Inns gave a general grounding in the codified systems of Roman and Canon law, but they were chiefly concerned with the ramshackle but extremely effective system of Common Law, based on precedents and cases rather than code and principle, which had emerged in Anglo-Saxon England, and which had since been added to, elucidated and extended by Parliamentary statute. All the practitioners in the assizes, and in the two Common Law high courts at Westminster, and all the royal judges except in Chancery, were drawn from the four principal Inns.

Yet the Inns were not simply colleges of the legal profession; they formed, in effect, an upper-class university of London. Landowners had to know something of the law to protect their estates. Moreover, from the fourteenth century, they were called increasingly, as unpaid Justices of the Peace, to administer the Common Law themselves. And, as members of Parliament, whether peers or Knights of the Shires, they belonged to a body which, unlike in France, was not composed of professional jurists, but of amateur politicians, but who nevertheless handled a great deal of legal business. So they sent their sons to the Inns. In the fifteenth century, a leading judge, Sir John Fortescue, wrote a book praising the English legal system, in which he did not fail to note, perhaps with the Templars in mind, that torture was not admissible in English law. He says of the Inns: 'Knights, barons and also other magnates and nobles of the realm place their sons in these Inns, although they do not intend them to be imbued with a professional knowledge of the laws, nor to live by its practice, but upon their patrimonies alone.' Indeed, he adds, it cost the student at least 20 marks (£13 6s 8d) a year to live in one of the Common Law Inns, 'Hence it comes about that there is scarcely a man learned in the laws to be found in the realm who is not noble or sprung of noble lineage.' The universities, he says, were no substitute, for they taught only in Latin; and the English law was conducted in a mixture of Latin, French and English. Therefore students had to be taught in what he terms 'a public academy', sited between the law-courts and City, in places where 'the tumult of the crowd' could not 'disturb the students' quiet'.

In the first flush of the Renaissance, there was a real possibility that the Continental, or Roman, system would oust the Common Law in England. Henry VIII's breach with the Church struck one blow at this tendency; but it was the massive resistance of the Common Law Inns, with their ramifying connections with the ruling class they had schooled, which proved conclusive. Indeed, the reign of Elizabeth saw the final triumph of the Common Law, and a corresponding rise in the numbers who flocked to its Inns. Lord Chancellor Hatton said in 1588: 'There are now more at the bar in one house than there were at all the Inns of Court when I was a young man.' So the four Common Law Inns gradually absorbed the Chancery Inns – Clement's, Clifford's, Lyons, the Staple, and so forth. The sons of peers and gentlemen sometimes went to Oxford or Cambridge first; nearly all attended an Inn, at least for a few terms: it was their first introduction not only to the business of law and government, but to court and London society. The great families had their favourite Inns: thus, the Cecils and the Bacons went to Gray's, generation after generation. Those students who were going to be professional lawyers spent six to nine years at their studies, reading and writing exercises in the morning, attending 'moots' and 'bolts' after dinner. Then they qualified as 'utter barristers', and ten years after being called to the bar, they became 'ancients' of their Inn, or Society as it was called, when they acquired, among other privileges, the right to choose their bedfellows (Elizabethans usually slept in pairs).

In Shakespeare's England the Inns were places of general culture, as well as legal studies. Ralegh signed his first poems 'Walter Ralegh of the Middle Temple'. Beaumont was at the Inner Temple, John Donne the preacher at Lincoln's Inn, Sir Philip Sidney was at Gray's. The Inns, in fact, played a notable part in the Elizabethan flowering, especially in the theatre. In the fifteenth century they had staged masks and other shows during the winter season of rejoicing, which stretched intermittently from Christmas to Shrovetide. There was a great feast for the judges and sergeants-at-law (equivalent to doctors in the universities) at Candlemass, 2 February; and after supper on every Saturday during the season, the Benchers danced the revels in their gowns, while the young barristers performed 'the measured galliard, etc., in very laudable manner, the Benchers beholding it'.

In the middle decades of the sixteenth century, hard times diminished these festivals. But in 1561, the Inner Temple wished to celebrate the end of an acrimonious dispute over property which they had had with the Middle Temple, and which they had won thanks to the vigorous support of Robert Dudley, Elizabeth's favourite. In gratitude, they laid down that no member of their Society was ever to plead in court against Dudley or his heirs, and they appointed him Constable-Marshall of their revels. They put on a performance which included a mask, and a play, *Gorboduc*, written by two of their members, the great parliamentary lawyer, Thomas Norton, and Thomas Sackville (later, as Lord Buckhurst, Elizabeth's last Treasurer, and builder of Knole). It was the first blank-verse tragedy ever written in England, and thus the immediate ancestor of Shakespeare's finest works. The Queen heard such praise of the performance that she had it staged again at Whitehall, and there (we surmise) she first saw Christopher Hatton, a young student at the Inner Temple, and its Master of the Game, dance the galliard. In time she made him Chancellor (which upset the professional lawyers), though he had first to serve a long apprenticeship, at court and in Parliament.

The Inns put on their own plays, written and performed by students and barristers; but they also hired professionals. Thus the diarist John Manningham of the Middle Temple notes that on 2 February 1602, to mark the completion of the splendid new dining hall (unhappily destroyed by the Nazis), a new play called *Twelfth Night* got its first performance 'at our feast'. Not everyone approved of these entertainments: Norton himself became a passionate opponent of plays in later life. Francis Bacon's puritan mother wrote: 'I trust they will not mum, masque nor sinfully revel at Gray's Inn.' Even at the Inner Temple, a more lax establishment than Gray's, there was a row in 1611 after a Candlemass play which was judged unsuitable. The Benchers laid down: 'For that great disorder and scurrility is brought into this House by lewd and lascivious plays, it is likewise ordered in this parliament that from henceforth there shall be no more plays in this House, either upon the feast of All Saints or Candlemass day, but the same from henceforth to be utterly taken away and abolished.' A concert and puppet-show was substituted; but the next year the plays were back again. Indeed, perhaps the most sumptuous performance of all was given at Shrovetide, 1613, to mark the marriage of James I's daughter. This was a joint production of the Middle Temple and Lincoln's Inn, and the top professionals were employed. And what professionals! The scenery, we are told, was 'by our Kingdome's most Artful and Ingenious Architect, Inigo Jones', and the text of the mask was 'Aplied, Digested and Written' by George Chapman. Manningham records that forty young barristers took part; and James I, a notorious homosexual, told them 'he never saw so many proper men together'. There were also 'a dozen little boys, dressed like baboons . . . the best show that hath been seen many a day'. As often happened with these legal shows, there were arguments and recriminations afterwards. The published text of the mask was a mess, Chapman angrily explaining to the reader that he was 'prevented by the unexpected haste of the printer, which he never let me know, and never sending me a proof till he had passed their speeches, I had no reason to imagine he could have been so forward'. He also complained of his fee: while others, he said, had been paid £50 for similar work, he had been 'put with taylors and shoomakers, and such snipperadoes, to be paid with a bill of particulars'. As a matter of fact, the production had cost each Inn over £1,000, raised by a levy on the members; and,

Middle Temple Hall, c. 1800.
It was here that the first
performance of *Twelfth Night*
took place.

being lawyers, some of them disputed the size of their individual contributions, and litigation was still going on twenty years later.

One great lawyer we can be certain was not present on this occasion was Sir Edward Coke, Lord Chief Justice and the Justinian of the English Common Law. His lifetime spanned the rise and decline of the entire Elizabethan and Jacobean drama; but Lord Campbell, in his *Lives of the Chief Justices*, writes of Coke 'it is supposed that in the whole course of his life he never saw a play acted, or read a play, or was in company with a player'. It was the law he took seriously. When he was a student at the Inner Temple, he rose at three, in the winter lighting his own fire. He then read legal textbooks and year-books until eight, when he went by water to Westminster, and heard cases argued until midday. He attended readings or lectures in the afternoon, resumed his private studies until supper, and afterwards took part in the moots – when difficult points of law were publicly debated – which were held in the garden by the river, or on rainy days in the covered walks near the Temple church. Coke was a grim, unlovable and sometimes savage man, who flogged his daughter when she declined to marry the brother of James's favourite and thus advance Coke in his profession. But his devotion to the law overrode every other consideration. Not only did he enormously improve the teaching of law in the Inner Temple, but his work in Parliament, on the Bench, and in compiling and editing cases, erected the Common Law virtually into a principal of government. No one else knew as much law as he, and he was able, in effect, to rewrite legal history to conform with his principles. But he established, once and for all, the theory that England is a government of laws, not of men, and that the crown itself is subject to Common Law and parliamentary statute. Thus, by his writings and by his example, he laid down the main ideological plank in the parliamentary platform against the Stuart tyranny. It was by virtue of his assumptions that Charles I was defied, humbled and eventually executed, his prerogative courts destroyed, and the House of Commons became the executive as well as the legislature. It was, indeed, the supremacy of the Common Lawyers in the Long Parliament which frustrated Cromwell's strenuous efforts to bring about a reform of the English legal system – which had to wait until the nineteenth century and beyond. On the other hand, what the Common Lawyers in the Coke tradition did establish was the fundamental liberties of the subject, enshrined in the Bill of Rights, thus forming the basis of the rule of law in Britain, the United States and virtually all other free countries.

In the eighteenth century, the Common Law Inns gradually ceased to be an alternative university, though both public and literary men continued to read there for a few terms. Lincoln's Inn enregistered many famous politicians, including William Pitt the Younger, Canning, Disraeli and Gladstone. The list of alumni of the two Temples is even more colourful: John Hampden, who studied under Coke, Clarendon who sided, *in extremis*, with the prerogative against the Common Law (though he lived to uphold it as Lord Chancellor), Judge Jeffreys who repudiated all the principles of English jurisprudence, John Evelyn, Wychery, Cowper, Congreve, Fielding, Burke, Sheridan, De Quincey and Thackeray. The Inns protected their liberties and franchises with persistent stubbornness (and sometimes – venom) over the centuries. As early as 1376, the Benchers of Lincoln's Inn had a man sent to prison for setting mantraps in their fields (now Lincoln's Inn Fields), for 'The King and Council have ever been very careful of preserving the liberties and interests of the lawyers and citizens in these fields, for their cure and refreshment'. Again, in 1613, the Council instructed London magistrates 'to restrayne and forbid' anyone who 'doe goe aboute to erect new buildings, contrary to His Majesty's Proclamation... and to the great pestring and annoyance of that Society'. If the Inns prevented others from building to their prejudice, they built or rebuilt themselves, when they chose, in legal defiance of City ordinances; even today, they do not require normal planning permission for their schemes. In one respect they have been liberal: until recently it was quite common (it still happens occasionally) for people who have no connection with the law to lease rooms in the Inns. Thus, Oliver Goldsmith lived at Number 2 Brick Court, in the Temple, where his parties disturbed the studies of the famous legal commentator Sir William Blackstone, whose chambers were below. Dr Johnson, a more acceptable tenant,

Sir William Blackstone, the great eighteenth-century jurist whose chambers were in the Temple.

Temple Bar, the west side.

TEMPLE BARR The Welt-Side

was at Number 1 Inner Temple Lane, from 1760 to 1765, and
there he received James Boswell, another student at the Temple
before he took up his practice at the Scottish bar.

The buildings in which Johnson lived were still standing in the
1820s when Sergeant Ballantine took chambers in the Inner
Temple, at Number 5. In his reminiscences, published in 1882,
he gave the place a bad name: 'Dirt seemed at that time an
attribute of the law.' 'I shared,' he wrote, 'with some half-dozen
other aspirants to the Bench what, in Temple parlance, is called
a laundress, probably from the fact of her never having washed
anything. I fancy that her principal employment was walking
from my chambers to the pawnbroker's, and thence to the gin-
shop . . . A mischievous little urchin cleaned my boots, and was
called a clerk.' He rejoiced when Inner Temple Lane was pulled
down in the 1850s, and replaced by a range called Dr Johnson's
Buildings. Not many of the old-style chambers remain today; but
a few have ancient (usually seventeenth-century) staircases,
panelled rooms and decorative fireplaces. A more impressive
reminder of the past are the rich collections of silver, accumulated
from Elizabethan times, which both societies still display in the
halls on feast-days: standing salts, spice-boxes, fruit-baskets and
dishes, candlesticks, snuffers and stands, tureens, salvers, bowls,
wine-cups, tankards, silver-mounted jugs, sauceboats and por-
ringers.

In 1855 a Royal Commission reported on the Inns of Court, and
as a result their procedures for admitting and examining candidates for the bar became more uniform and efficient, though they

have changed comparatively little in the last century or so. An
Inn need not assign its reasons for rejecting a student, but
normally he is called to the bar without much difficulty provided
he has 'kept' the requisite nine terms by 'eating his dinners' in
the Hall of the Inn. The Middle Temple summons its members to
dinner on a hunting horn; the Inner Temple uses a silver-mounted
ram's horn; otherwise there is not much difference to the casual
observer, though the symbol of the first is a Lamb and Flag, the
second a Winged Horse. The real business of learning the law
begins when a student is 'called', and works in chambers under a
senior barrister, 'deviling' and hoping for briefs. The Inns do not
train solicitors, who can plead only at Crown courts and petty
sessions, and before inferior judges. Barristers, by contrast, as
members of the bar are, strictly speaking, officers of the court;

King's Bench Walk in the
Middle Temple.

their prime duty, indeed, is to the law, rather than the client. This status, which dates from the later part of the Middle Ages, has a number of important and jealously-preserved consequences. The fee they are paid through solicitors for undertaking a case is endorsed on their brief and payable afterwards; it is not a contract, recoverable at law, but a *quiddam honorarium*, in origins a kind of legalized bribe, which a client paid to counsel, as an officer of the law, to expedite his affairs. Thus a barrister cannot normally sue to recover money, unless it has already been paid over to the solicitor who briefs him. On the other hand, a barrister enjoys compensating privileges. He cannot, unlike a solicitor, be sued by a client for damages as a result of professional negligence. He can claim absolute control of all litigation in which he is engaged, and may even withdraw it from court, unless the client expressly dissents. Nor is he answerable in law for false information supplied to him, unless of course he has invented it himself, in which case he falls within the shadow of the First Statute of Westminster, of the third year of the reign of King Edward I, Chapter 29 (or, as the pundits put it, 3 Ed. I., chap. 29), though the punishment now is disbarring, sentence being awarded not, as in the past, by the Benchers of individual Inns, but by the Bar Council. Junior counsel wear a stuff gown and a small wig. In due course, they can take the risk of applying to the Lord Chancellor for the title of Queen's Counsel. It is not always granted, though barrister-MPs are notoriously more fortunate than others; nor, when granted, is it always wise; a successful junior counsel sometimes finds that his income drops, at least initially, as a QC. As a 'counsel learned in the law', however, he is in the top section of his profession, wears a silk gown, and on state occasions – and invariably in the House of Lords – a full-bottomed wig. Only a 'silk' can hope for the major prizes of his profession: the superior judgeships, the High Court and Court of Appeals, the law offices of the Crown, the Chancellorship, the right to be elected Bencher or officer of his Inn. The law is a very hierarchical business indeed.

The Temple Inns of Court have few cobwebs these days; their routines and traditions, though cherished, are meretricious rather than fundamental to the work they do. They are international in outlook, taking students from the scores of Commonwealth and foreign countries which have been influenced by English jurisprudence. They may become more internationalist still, if Britain remains a member of the European Economic Community, for Community law is in the tradition of Roman jurisprudence and the Napoleonic Code – the antithesis, in many ways, of the Common Law system which the Inns of Court defended so triumphantly in the sixteenth and seventeenth centuries. The English law, and the Inns with it, thus face the biggest revolution in their history. In many respects they will not like it; but past history suggests that, whatever happens, the Inns will maintain the central and privileged position they have held in our legal system for over five centuries.

Berkeley Castle today –
partially rebuilt by the last
Earl of Berkeley who showed
'a total want of respect for
the truth of architectural
history'.

7 BERKELEY CASTLE
Keeping it in the Family

No OTHER CASTLE in England has such a menacing silhouette as Berkeley in Gloucestershire. Seen from the Severn water-meadows, especially on a misty morning, it rises, phantom-like, a great, man-made cliff of stone. There is terror in these harsh walls and battlements; but also a strange beauty. Berkeley is built chiefly of sandstone from the Severn banks, of a rare, rose-petal pink. Interlacing these sandstone blocks are thin slabs of grey tufa, or pumicestone; and over the walls creeps the red valerian. The weather, the seasons, the varying times of day, subject the castle to a constant metamorphosis: sometimes it is pink, sometimes grey, sometimes both at once; in certain lights it turns to deep purple. Berkeley is a military fortification which has assumed, over many centuries, some of the aspects of a great country house. But it keeps its martial air; no one who gazes up at it from below, or tramps its walls, can be in any doubt that here is a place built to keep the multitudes in subjection and, if necessary, harbour the recalcitrant in its dungeons. It is an artefact of the feudal life-style.

On 27 July 1399, Henry, Duke of Lancaster, met Edmund of York at Berkeley to plan the overthrow of King Richard II, and so set in motion the chain of events which led to the Wars of the Roses. Shakespeare set the scene:

> There stands the castle, by yon tuft of trees,
> Mann'd with three hundred men.

How far the castle of those days resembled the building we can see today is a matter of conjecture. In essence, Berkeley is a late-Norman fortress, about 1156, with a scarped ovoid shell-keep, sixty-two feet above base-level, and with two wards, on each side of it, linked by a gateway. The size of the mound on which the keep rests indicates that there was an earlier, more primitive Norman fort on the site; and it is likely that the place was defended long before the Normans came, for the Vale of Berkeley has always been rich agricultural land, and throughout the Dark Ages it was necessary to protect it against Welsh marauders from across the Severn. Berkeley, so far as we know, has never been a ruin. From the twelfth century at least it has been in continuous occupation, and successive generations enlarged, strengthened, altered and restored its walls and rooms, leaving, in most cases, no written records of what they did. Even in the twentieth century, there have been major changes, for the last Earl of Berkeley, who inherited the castle in 1916, rebuilt many of its feudal features, bringing to the work, as one historian has put it, 'considerable taste and knowledge, ample means, and a total want of respect for the truth of architectural history'. From other ancient houses he acquired, and installed at Berkeley, a vast fireplace, an oak screen and a fourteenth-century gatehouse. Thus the castle is an amalgam of the true past and romantic antiquarianism, and much of what we are told about it is legend or guesswork.

What makes Berkeley unique is not so much the continuity of the fabric as the extraordinary tenacity with which the Berkeley family has clung to it. There is still a Berkeley at the castle, and he can trace his line of descent, without too much exercise of historical imagination, back to before the Conquest. Only half a dozen families in England can do the same; and none now occupies the same ground as its distant ancestors. Truly ancient lineage is a very rare thing. In the last quarter of the nineteenth century, professional genealogical historians, led by the ferocious J. H. Round, carried out a vast work of demolition on the pedigrees of English noble houses; few emerged without damage, usually conclusive, to their claims. Being a great landowning magnate in Medieval England was a precarious profession: it was most exceptional for a family to stay at the top for more than three or four generations. Death in battle, plague, political mis-calculation – leading to execution and forfeiture – extinguished many. Others, the majority in fact, disappeared by failing to provide male heirs. There was always a temptation to replenish their fortunes by marrying heiresses, and this increased the genetic chances of a failure of males: thus a marriage which saved an estate in one generation often led to its eclipse in the next. The convulsions of the sixteenth and seventeenth centuries, from which the bulk of the English aristocracy date their origins, saw the destruction of nearly all of the remaining Medieval magnate-families. As long ago as 1626 Lord Chief Justice Crew asked rhetorically in court: 'Where is Bohun? Where's Mobray? Where's Mortimer? Nay, which is more, and most of all, where is Plantagenet?' They were all since long gone, and scores of other historic names with them. But the Berkeleys could answer Justice Crew from their castle. And, more surprisingly still, they are around 350 years later to invalidate his scepticism.

When William 1, victor in battle, was accepted as king by the Anglo-Saxon nobility, and crowned at Westminster, he seems to have intended to avoid a mass-confiscation of estates, and to associate the leaders of Saxon society with his rule. But a series of rebellions led him to change his policy and Domesday Book, at the end of his reign, records an almost total change of land-ownership at the top. The few survivors were second-rank men, who collaborated with the Occupation, and changed their names to the French style. The Berkeleys were among them, as were the Cromwells, the Lumleys, the Greystokes, the Audleys and the Fitzwilliams. Eadnoth the Staller was a government official under Edward the Confessor, but fought for the Conqueror after Hastings. His son called himself Harding, and his grandson Fitzharding; and it was a younger brother of this last, Robert Fitzharding, a merchant and reeve of Bristol, who made himself useful to the future Henry II by lending him money during the anarchy of King Stephen's reign. By a charter of 1149 he was awarded part of the manor of Berkeley, and by a further charter in 1154 the remainder. The original owners of the manor were appeased by a double marriage into the Fitzhardings, but it was the Fitzharding blood – now renamed Berkeley – which surfaced.

Much of our knowledge of the family derives from the prodigious researches of one John Smythe of Nibley, who was born on the estate in 1567 and managed the Berkeley family's affairs for many years. Smythe tells us he was 'for four and thirty years a professional ploughman, having all that time eaten much of my bread from the labours of my own hands'. But he was also a passionate antiquary, who in addition to his work as Berkeley steward roved all over England consulting and acquiring records, and amassing material about the ancient family he served. He left a mass of papers dealing with such matters as 'The Rules for the Keeping of my Clock', but including also the manuscript of his *Lives of the Berkeleys*, which was finally published, in three volumes, in 1883–5. He wrote: 'I have represented all things truly', adding:

The custom of those who write histories is to propose in the beginning a model of the subject they mean to handle. Mine is, of noble men and noble minds, whom I will not celebrate above their merit: stand or stoop, they shall unto themselves. Labour I will through all the months 550 years to reflect to this family the image of itself, in all or the more remarkable actions or accidents, chances and changes, which in the reigns of 24 princes of this English monarchy have fallen upon the descendants thereof.

Smythe saw the Berkeleys as a dynasty, like the kings themselves; and he gives the head of the house in each generation a number or nickname – Thomas the Wise, Maurice the Magnanimous, Thomas the Magnificent, and so forth. One of his themes is the effect of individual character and capacity on the fortunes of the house; and, too, the varying effectiveness of those Berkeleys who chose to fight for power by the sword, and those who preferred the law. He notes William of Malmesbury's judgment on Robert Fitzharding, the real founder of the estate: 'he was more accustomed to sharpen his tongue for litigious ends than to make steel clash on steel in battle'. A wise fellow – wiser than his

The dungeon where, according to tradition, Edward II was murdered after the *coup* of Mortimer and Isabella.

descendant, Robert II, who nearly lost the barony by leaguing himself against King John. Of his brother and successor, Thomas I, Smythe says: 'He so evenly observed a prudent inclining after the strongest powers, that he ever avoided those Court and Country storms, which in his time blew down many stronger cedars than himself.' Thomas II was '28 times in the field', surviving the disaster of Bannockburn. His son, Maurice III, broke with Edward II and died a prisoner in Wallingford Castle. Such treatment was amply revenged. Edward's estranged French wife, Isabella, took as her lover Roger Mortimer, Earl of March, and Maurice's son and heir, Thomas III, was a member of Mortimer's faction, for he had married his sister. When Edward was captured by Mortimer, he was handed to Thomas's keeping at Berkeley and later it was announced he was dead.

Some mystery still surrounds this crime. The young King Edward III made only perfunctory efforts to identify and punish his father's murderers. Thomas claimed he was away from the castle when the King died; but Smythe was able to show, from the documents, that this was untrue. There were no marks on Edward II's body and he was buried with great solemnity in Gloucester Abbey under an alabaster effigy and a fine stone canopy, which survive today. Some said he had been smothered or starved to death, and at Berkeley today they show you a pit-dungeon in which, it is claimed, he was kept, the diseased carcases of dead cattle being thrown in alongside him, so he would be asphyxiated by the stench. But Edward was a man of fine physique, a great athlete, and he did not die easily. Many years later, John of Trevisa, who had been a boy in Berkeley town at the time (he was later chaplain to the castle), translated Ranulf de Higden's *Polychronicon* into English, and interpolated historical material from his own knowledge. He states flatly that the King was killed 'with a hoote broche putte thro the secret place posteriale'. This confirms the ancient story that Edward died a horrible death from a red-hot poker, and that his screams set the castle dogs barking (there is even a tale that they could be heard in Berkeley town, though this seems almost inconceivable). In the eighteenth century Thomas Gray conjured up the scene:

> Weave the warp and weave the woof,
> The winding-sheet of Edward's race;
> Give ample room and verge enough,
> The characters of Hell to trace.
> Mark the year and mark the night,
> When Severn shall re-echo with the affright,
> The shrieks of death through Berkeley's roof that ring,
> Shrieks of an agonising king.

All the same, the dead king's son found it convenient to accept Thomas III's explanation, and this Berkeley lord lived to become, as Smythe puts it, 'a great lord and landmongre', marrying a rich

Below Effigy of Edward II in Gloucester Cathedral.

widow 'fruitful to her husband in both lands and children'. Both Thomas, and his heir Maurice IV, fought at Poitiers, though the latter never really recovered from the wounds he received there. The reeve of one Berkeley manor 'spent three quarters and seven bushels of beans in fatting one hundred geese towards his funeral'.

In Medieval times, a great landed house could not stand still: to survive it had to expand, and expansion meant dabbling in politics, with the risks of incurring royal hatred, or the enmity of other powerful houses. In the early fifteenth century, the Berkeleys expanded by acquiring the Lisle inheritance: but this led to lawsuits and fighting for nearly two hundred years. When the head of the Talbots, Earls of Shrewsbury, who also claimed the Lisle lands served a subpoena on James, Lord Berkeley, the latter forced the messenger to eat it, parchment, seals and all; as a result, there was an assault on Berkeley town, which, said Smythe, never recovered 'from the burning and prostration of many of her ancient houses'. In 1470 Viscount Lisle challenged William, Lord Berkeley, to meet him in combat at Nibley Green. It has some

According to William of Malmesbury, Berkeley once had a witch, who at the end of her life regretted her wicked deeds and exhorted her children (a monk and a nun) to do all they could to safeguard her soul in death. Despite their immense precautions, the Devil came to claim her, snapped the thick chains binding the coffin, and carried her off. This picture is a fifteenth-century print from Nuremberg, showing the Devil taking her away.

claims to be considered the last purely private battle in England, and the Berkeleys won it – Lisle was shot through the face by an arrow and finished off with a dagger. But William, partly to protect himself from the consequences of the feud and partly to spite his brother and heir, came to an arrangement with King Henry VII, under which the castle and most of his estate was entailed on the King, in return for a marquisate. This was the highest point the Berkeleys ever reached in the peerage and as a result of the deal the castle passed out of their hands, for the first and last time, for more than a generation: hence Smythe's nickname, 'William the Waste-All'. Maurice V became an amateur lawyer to repair some of the damage his brother had inflicted on the family fortunes. Smythe gives a little vignette of him 'with a milk-white head in his irksome old age, in Winter terms and frosty seasons, with a buckram bag stuffed with law cases, in early mornings and late evenings, walking with his eldest son between the four Inns of Court and Westminster Hall, following his law suits in his own old person'.

The lawsuits continued throughout Queen Elizabeth's reign, and under adverse conditions, for the Lisle claim had devolved upon the rapacious Dudleys, one of whom, Robert, Earl of Leicester, was the Queen's greatest friend. The head of the house, whom Smythe calls 'Henry the Harmless', made matters worse by marrying a Howard, sister of the Fourth Duke of Norfolk, executed for treason in 1572. This meant, in effect, that the Berkeleys were not only excluded from court favour, but became objects of suspicion. In 1574, during a royal progress through the West Country, Leicester arranged for the court to stop at Berkeley during Henry's absence, and hunt his deer. Henry discovered on his return, that twenty-seven had been slaughtered, and threatened to dispark the enclosure. Leicester represented this threat to the queen as a personal insult to her, and in the row that followed Henry risked losing his liberty as well as his estate. He was not so much harmless as improvident. Though his income was diminished and encumbered, he kept 150 servants in his household and expected 300 tenants on horseback to greet him whenever he passed through Berkeley town: this was foolish behaviour for a man who could not hope to get his hands on the profits of any government office. In the end, Henry was forced to sell off lands worth £42,000, but at least he protected the remains of the property by coming to a settlement with Lord Lisle in 1609 – thus ending a battle which had lasted 192 years and had cost more than four times the value of the lands at stake.

Henry's successor, George, retrenched by travelling abroad and marrying an heiress. But such arranged marriages were liable to create difficulties and expense of their own. George's wife objected strongly to his using her inheritance to pay off his debts, accompanied as it was by a refusal to live with her. A reproachful letter from her has survived, with George's furious reply scribbled on the back:

DR GEORGE BERKELEY BISHOP OF CLOYNE

THIS
HOLY
BIBLE

MINUTE PHILOSOPHER
SIRIS

Bishop Berkeley, a major
figure of the empirical school
of British philosophy.

. . . since I find you have neither obedience nor love, but that you will
be the overthrow of both me and my posterity, I hold you to be so
unworthy a wife, that I am determined for many years not to come near
you, but seek my fortune in other places, and whatsoever becomes of me,
I will let the world know you are the cause of it, in being so undutiful a
wife, so fare well.

But George at least had the sense to decline to fight for the king
during the Civil War; he stayed in London with the Parliament
and his passive role was not held against him by the Royalists,
especially since his son took a leading part in restoring Charles II
to his throne. Indeed, the Berkeleys played a prudent hand during
these difficult years, for this same son sided with the bulk of the
Whig nobility in turning out James II in 1688, ending his life as
Earl of Berkeley. The eighteenth century was a prosperous
period for the family, and in some ways a distinguished one. They
produced Bishop Berkeley, the philosopher; a Chief Justice of
Ireland (admittedly described by Swift as 'intolerably lazy') and
a famous admiral. The last, Lord James, was the subject of one of
Hervey's sharp pen-portraits:

. . . rough, proud, hard and obstinate, with excellent good natural parts,
but so uncultivated that he was totally ignorant of every branch of
knowledge except his profession. He was haughty and tyrannical, but
honourable; gallant, observant of his word, but equally incapable of
flattering a prince, bending to a minister, or lying to anybody he had
to deal with.

From their castle, the Berkeleys dispensed parliamentary
patronage, sometimes sending four members of their family to the
Commons. For generations, they upheld the Whig cause in the
locality, against the Tory forces of the Dukes of Beaufort. But sometimes, to save the enormous cost of contested elections, the two
parties signed a truce, and each took one of the two county seats.
In 1783 Beaufort put out a statement that 'His Grace and Lord
Berkeley have settled the Peace of the County of Gloucestershire
as far as lay in their power by Mutually Agreeing to One and One,
so that Mr Geo. Berkeley is to come in without any opposition.
These conditions are such in his Opinion as cannot fail of Meeting
with the Approbation of all parties'.

Besides borough-mongering, the Beauforts and the Berkeleys
shared another passion: hunting. The Berkeleys had always been
great huntsmen, and had run a private pack of hounds since fox-
hunting came into fashion after the Civil War, dressing their
servants in spectacular yellow coats. But Frederick Augustus,
the Fifth Earl, was the grandest sportsman of all. He worked his
hounds continuously throughout the season, moving by stages
from Berkeley to Charing Cross, and then back again, killing foxes
all the way. When, in time, he found this procedure too strenuous,
he split his hounds into two packs: one became the Old Berkeley,
which since then has hunted in the Vale of Aylesbury, while the
Berkeley itself was based, as it still is, at the castle.

'The Berkeleys had always been great huntsmen and had run a private pack of hounds since fox-hunting came into fashion after the Civil War.'

Frederick Augustus achieved notoriety by killing a highwayman, and a measure of real fame by patronizing the efforts of a local doctor, Edward Jenner, to pioneer vaccination against smallpox. Unfortunately, he was also a systematic seducer of young girls, whom he refused to marry when he got them pregnant: 'They will never get the chain round my neck', he boasted. At the age of forty he triumphed over one Mary Cole, the seventeen-year-old daughter of a local butcher, but it was at this point he met his match. Mary moved into the castle, bore her lord seven children, took over the management of the estates, and in 1796 got the Earl to marry her: his brother told him, 'If you had chosen from a throne you might perhaps not have got a better.' But the belated marriage, which was followed by more children, placed the eldest bastard son, who had been brought up as the heir, in an invidious position. In 1234, a Lord Berkeley had been present at the parliament held at Merton. There, he and the other barons had rejected a demand by the clergy that children born before the marriage of their parents should be declared legitimate; they called out with one voice, 'No. We refuse to change the laws of England!' The matter was finally put right in 1926, but in 1796 the Fifth Earl found he could not legitimize his eldest son. He could leave him the castle and the estates, but not the earldom; nor could the son inherit six large parcels of land, and twenty priceless acres of Mayfair, including Berkeley Square, which had been willed to the legal heir by a distant kinsman.

In desperation, and no doubt prompted by the masterful Mary, the Earl forged a series of entries in the register of Berkeley parish church, 'proving' that he and his wife had been secretly married as long ago as 1785. The case went to law, and eventually to the House of Lords, and after a generation of argument – providing the basis for Dickens's Jarndyce v Jarndyce in *Bleak House*

– the claim that the earlier marriage had taken place was unanimously dismissed by the peers. Some curious glimpses of the life of the aristocracy in the eighteenth century, and the Fifth Earl's methods of seduction, are provided in *A Narrative of the Minutes of Evidence respecting the Claim to the Berkeley Peerage*, published in London in 1811. Frederick Augustus and Mary were lucky not to be prosecuted for forgery; lesser folk would have been hanged or transported. As it was, the legitimate heir, Thomas Morton, behaved with astonishing forebearance; he could not decline the title, but he deliberately remained unmarried, and he made over to his eldest brother the London estates, worth £18,000 a year – for which he got scant thanks. The Fifth Earl died in 1810, leaving a will disinheriting any of his children who doubted the validity of his earlier 'marriage'; and Mary survived him thirty-four years to keep the family up to scratch on the point. Whether the eldest son, William Fitzharding, was worth all this effort and risk is very doubtful. By his borough-mongering

Right Grantley Fitzharding Berkeley MP, a great and dangerous eccentric who once horsewhipped the publisher of a magazine which reviewed his book unfavourably.

A peaceful setting for the present Berkeley descendants – but there was once 'terror in these harsh walls and battlements'.

service to the Whigs, he won the title of Earl Fitzharding. But the diarist Charles Greville, Clerk to the Privy Council, dismissed him as 'an arrant blackguard . . . notorious for general worthlessness'. Lascivious like his father, he failed to produce any heir at all, and the title died with him.

Mary's sons, legitimate or otherwise, illustrated John Smythe's point that the Berkeleys tended to be either cautious conciliators, or hotheaded to the point of folly. Grantley Fitzharding, MP for Berkeley, fell into the latter category. He wrote a three-volume novel about his birthplace, *Berkeley Castle*, which was unfavourably reviewed in *Fraser's Magazine*. Assisted by one of his brothers, he horsewhipped the publisher, and then fought a duel with the reviewer, after which he was fined £100 for assault. Later, he spent £30,000 defending his parliamentary seat against one of his brothers, and he seems to have relished a fight against any opponent, and on whatever terrain. Victorian society knew him as a great and dangerous eccentric, the last man in England, when he died in 1881, to wear an old-fashioned flat cocked hat. He learned boxing from Byron's instructor, 'Gentleman Jim' Jackson, wrote volumes of poetry and travel, as well as novels, a book on potato blight, and a pamphlet asserting that animals were as good as men. His own beasts were famous: his terrier Smike, his bloodhound Druid, his mastiff Grumbo, and his retriever Smoker; and he tamed and kept a cormorant called Jack. He survives through his three-volume autobiography, *Reminiscences of a Sportsman*, illustrated by John Leech, which is a classic of its kind.

Another one of Mary's sons received a peerage, as Lord Fitzharding of Bristol; and his heir, the Second Baron, earned our gratitude by allowing Smythe's manuscript *Lives* to be published – 'the only concession to historical research', as a historian recently put it, 'the Berkeleys have ever made'. The *Lives* is a great book, perhaps the finest family history ever written in England, learned, eccentric and highly readable, the story not only of a remarkable family, but of the fields and woods they owned. It is a pity that no modern Smythe has arisen to record the later centuries of the story, for the Berkeleys continued to illustrate the fickleness of fortune, and the dramatic interplay of men and events. No *Forsyte Saga* in fiction can rival their history in sheer human interest. In 1916, death and accident brought the earldom of the legitimate line back to Berkeley Castle. Among other things, the last earl was an expert on osmotic pressure, and a leading amateur golfer, author of *Sound Golf*; also, as we have already seen, a dedicated, if ruthless, castle-restorer. But he died childless, despite two marriages, and the old earldom and titles died with him. By his will, a curious and complex affair, the castle and the remains of the estate went to a junior descendant of Lord James, who had forced the hapless messenger to eat his subpoena. Thus a Berkeley still holds the castle, and Berkeleys still hunt in yellow coats from its gates.

For all its long history, Berkeley itself has been remarkably fortunate in its military encounters. It fell only once, to Cromwell's men in the 1640s; and, amazingly, it was not 'slighted' in consequence. The Commonwealth forces usually pulled down castles which had resisted them, but Berkeley was spared on condition that a breach they had made in the walls was never restored – and so it remains today. This was a stroke of pure luck. Indeed, the history of the Berkeleys indicates the extent to which blind chance determines the survival or extinction of an ancient house. The latest historian of the family, Professor Lawrence Stone, concludes his survey of its affairs in the sixteenth and seventeenth centuries by remarking, of its ups and downs, 'the determining factor was luck'. But the fact that members of the family still live in their castle, when so many other famous houses have vanished or linger in exile, suggests that, for all their misfortunes, the Berkeleys have had more luck than most. It is a theme, perhaps, for an English Tolstoy.

8 NORWICH

The Provincial Presence

ANYONE ATTEMPTING to select the ideal English provincial city would be strongly tempted to award the palm to Norwich. It was a place of considerable size and importance even when William the Conqueror came to England. With its 1,300 burghers it was, after York, the largest English town outside London and this was one reason why the Normans – in accordance with their ecclesiastical policy of transferring cathedrals from the rural areas where the Saxons had placed them – made Norwich, instead of Thetford, the seat of the East Anglian diocese. Bishop Herbert of Losinga, a cultured and masterful churchman from Lorraine, began to construct his new cathedral in 1096 and over the next fifty years it slowly emerged as one of the largest and most impressive Norman-Romanesque structures in the country. It is still essentially, like Durham and Peterborough, a Norman church and a striking testament to the ambition, even audacity, of its early-twelfth-century architects and stonemasons. But, like most of our cathedrals, it was enlarged, repaired and embellished over more than four centuries; the choir and the apse, in particular, display the majesty of fifteenth-century Perpendicular – England's greatest single contribution to architecture – soaring high above the earlier Norman columns. This lierne vault, as it is called, was the work of Walter Lyhart, bishop between 1446 and 1472, and his rebus of a stag lying in water was carved at the top of every alternate shaft of the vault. The vault is more a wall of glass than of stone, and Lyhart's successors reinforced and protected this fragile glass shell – for that is what it is – by graceful flying buttresses, severely functional in purpose but brilliant in their aesthetic impact, for they give the apse the impression of a gigantic tent which only the buttresses, like guy-ropes, prevent from floating into the wide Norfolk skies.

Indeed, considering the long centuries over which the cathedral rose, its apparent unity of concept and execution is astonishing. Medieval designers and craftsmen appear to have had the precious gift – now lost, alas – of superimposing the vernacular modes of their times on the work of their ancestors without the

Left Norwich cathedral – 'a striking testament to the ambition, even audacity, of its early twelfth-century architects'.

Right Norwich cathedral; the interior showing the pulpit and majestic fifteenth-century choir and apse.

slightest appearance of incongruity or disharmony. The immense length of the building – over four hundred feet – might have given the impression of disproportion, even indiscipline. But the concept is not only saved, but superbly vindicated by the dramatic spire, itself firmly placed on a tower of great deliberative strength, which is 315 feet high, and seems to rise into the stratosphere. What makes Norwich Cathedral so successful is the way its man-made silhouette both reflects and transfigures the natural landscape in which it is set: the long nave mirrors the interminable flatness of the Norfolk plain, while the arrow-like spire pierces, and so dramatizes, the vastness of the Norfolk sky. In a county of low horizons and Himalayan clouds, the cathedral is a penetrating comment on the relationship between man and the universe.

The cathedral dominates the town, as at Durham and Lincoln; and this is right. But there is much more to Norwich. For the

The Norwich Retable
showing (*left*) *Christ on the
Way to Calvary* and (*right*)
The Flagellation.

Castle, though an early Norman keep, square, simple and un-compromising in its basic lines, as befits a fortification made for military use and menace, is itself embellished with a gossamer design of blank arcading, as though its soldier-architects were not content to display strength alone but felt compelled to demon-strate their decorative skills to the glory of the science of war – just as the cathedral glorifies the Deity. Under the protection of the castle, the wealth of Norwich increased, especially after Edward III, as part of his deliberate policy of transforming England from a producer of wool into a textile-manufacturing country, trans-planted communities of Flemish weavers.

Norwich became a leading cloth town centuries before the Industrial Revolution brought wealth to Lancashire and York-shire; and this is reflected in the buildings which its citizens raised both for sacred and profane uses. The heart of old Norwich, protected on one side by its river, on the other by its city walls, is still a Medieval burgh: it has, perhaps, more pre-Renaissance houses (often concealed behind sixteenth- and seventeenth-century façades), than any other town in the kingdom, and no less than thirty-two Medieval parish churches. They are predomin-antly Perpendicular, but they cover the whole range of English styles and periods, local architectural manners, and the eccentrici-ties and inspirations of scores of unknown master-builders. The very names of these churches compose a litany evoking the Age of Faith, when a man's first loyalty, in spiritual matters no less than secular, was to his parish and its lovingly-embellished temple: St Clement Colegate, St Etheldreda, St George Tombland, St Gregory Pottergate, St John Baptist, St Giles, and St John Baptist Timberhill, St John de Sepulchre, St John Maddermarket, St Martin-at-Oak and St Martin-at-Palace, St Michael-at-Coslany, St Michael-at-Plea, and St Michael-at-Thorn, St Peter Mancroft and St Peter Permountgate. Wandering through these ancient churches – there were once, indeed, some twenty more – or walking through the narrow streets of Elm Hill, one comes closer to visualizing what it was actually like to live in a medieval city than anywhere else in England. One gets, too, the strong im-pression that this square mile or so of urban ground was much venerated and fiercely extolled by those who lived on it: they believed, and they boasted, that they were citizens of the finest town in the kingdom.

Loyalty, unreasoning and protective, has been a key emotion in the history of Norwich: loyalty to the parish, to the city itself, to the county and the countryside. The place is provincial in the best sense, lacking that feeling of inferiority towards the metro-polis, and towards national standards of sophistication and cul-ture, which demeans so many other county towns. The Norwich men cast no envious eyes towards London, feeling that they had created something at least as fine in quality, if not in size; that they had a local and civilized way of life which need fear no compar-ison and which was very much *sui generis*. When metropolitan government became intolerably oppressive, they took to arms and marched south, emboldened by ancient memories of independence and self-rule. The men of Norwich and the surrounding villages formed the hard core and the leadership of that great provincial confederation of 1381 which we call the Peasants' Revolt. Norfolk had been absorbed into the Mercian state long before King Alfred made Wessex the base of the first united English kingdom. But in 1381 the angry men of Norwich spoke of creating 'county kings', and referred in their manifestos to the 'Northfolk' – thus delving atavistically into capacious tribal memories which went back to a period even before the heptarchy of early Anglo-Saxon England, to a time when Norfolk was a kingdom in its own right, and the magnificent funeral treasures of Sutton Hoo were buried in a royal ship-cenotaph. The Norfolk men were 'out' again in 1549 under Kett; and in 1553 it was to Norfolk that Queen Mary Tudor – defying the Duke of Northumberland's attempt to place Lady Jane Grey on the throne – turned for refuge and support. At Norwich she set up her headquarters; the local gentry and their tenants flocked to her in arms; and it was at Norwich she received the news of Northumberland's ignominious capitulation.

The provincial separatism of the place, the refusal, generation after generation, to accept without protest the *diktat* of London, was underpinned by the existence of local centres of aristocratic power. The happy survival of that unique collection of intimate correspondence, the *Paston Letters*, gives us glimpses not merely into the daily lives of fifteenth-century Norfolk gentry, but into the legal and military conditions which made Norwich so remote from the capital, so accustomed to settle its own affairs by force or compromise on the spot.

Not that Norfolk was a backward place: its city was the second or third richest in the kingdom; the countryside was heavily populated by the standards of the time, well-farmed and fertile. These very facts enhanced its independent-mindedness, which survived well into the second half of the sixteenth century. Indeed, it was the only part of England south of the Trent and west of the Severn which still contained, even in Queen Elizabeth's time, a semi-independent Medieval domain. The Fourth Duke of Norfolk was the last duke of the old creation. In Norfolk, from his huge and rambling castle-house at Kenninghall, he ruled a self-contained empire of six hundred square miles with its own liberties, franchises and courts, where the writ of the crown, except in certain capital cases, did not run. Kenninghall was the largest palace in England, next to Hampton Court, and in Norwich itself he rebuilt, on a splendid scale, a Renaissance town mansion, equipped with its own chapel, tennis-courts, playhouse and bowling-alley – the first in England outside London. He owned much of the city and engineered the accommodation of a second great wave of emigrant Flemish artisans, driven from their homes in the Low Countries by the 'Spanish Fury' of Alva. When

Elm Hill, a street which still preserves something of the air of a medieval city.

Elizabeth accused Norfolk of plotting to marry Mary Queen of Scots, he protested he had no need to ally himself with royalty: 'When I am in my bowling-alley in Norwich,' he said proudly, 'I feel myself as good as many kings.'

Yet he plotted all the same, if with irresolution and incompetence, and Elizabeth duly chopped off his head in 1572. This time the men of Norwich and Norfolk did not rise, with the exception of a few local wastrels. Local patriots they were, but national patriots too, and sensible judges of what was in their interests.

They were well able to evaluate the respective merits of a foolish and vain duke, and an outstanding English monarch. Even so, when Elizabeth herself paid a state visit to Norwich during her summer progress of 1578, she was relieved and delighted at the warmth of her reception. The city had been at immense pains (and expense) to demonstrate its loyalty and regard for her. Though she was lodged at the Bishop's Palace, two miles outside the walls, the streets were cleansed, houses and public buildings repainted, and efforts made to keep the city sweet, for Elizabeth was notorious for her hatred of smells. 'No cows,' the city court laid down on 20 June, 'are to be brought into the city; no scourers to use any wash; no grocer to dry any tallow, etc, during her Majesty's abode here.' The poet and theatrical impresario Thomas Churchyard was hired to write and present pageants, and spent three weeks rehearsing the city waits and children (he also left a full account of the visit, sold in thousands as a penny pamphlet). Elizabeth responded magnificently, as she well knew how to do. When she arrived, on 16 August, and was presented with the customary gift of gold, she replied: 'We heartily thank

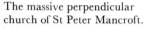

The massive perpendicular church of St Peter Mancroft.

you, Mr Mayor, and all the rest, for these tokens of good will. Nevertheless, princes have no need of money: God hath endowed us abundantly, we came not therefore but for that which in right is our own, the hearts and true allegiance of our subjects, which are the greatest riches of our kingdom.' She spent hours touring the city workshops, 'greatly admiring the nimble fingers' of the children at their knitting-frames; and when some of Churchyard's shows were almost crowded out by a busy timetable, she insisted on seeing them, to his abundant gratification. She told the city orator, Stephen Limbert, who ran the grammar-school, that his speech was 'the best that ever I heard', summoned the ambassadors and privy counsellors of her suite, 'and willed them to hearken, and she herself was very attentive'. When she finally left, she halted her horse at the city boundary and said: 'I shall never forget Norwich.' Then 'she shook her riding-whip and said "Farewell, Norwich", with the water standing in her eyes'.

Elizabeth was shrewd enough to appreciate not only the regard of the citizens but the fact that Norwich was one of the most adventurous cities in her kingdom, and not just by virtue of its industry. During her reign, Norwich was the first city outside London to hold free public concerts of music, once a week on summer evenings. Norwich choristers and musicians were famous, and seven of them accompanied Drake on his successful expedition to Portugal and the Azores in 1589; he was accustomed, as one of his Spanish prisoners tells us, 'to dine to the music of viols'. In some ways, indeed, Elizabethan Norwich was ahead of the capital in civic pride and forethought. During the 1570s it introduced the first comprehensive system of poor-relief, paid for by the rates, which became the model for London, indeed of the statutory provisions for the whole nation – and thus the distant ancestor of the modern welfare state.

The loyalty of Norwich to the prudent and tolerant Queen Elizabeth – who did not wish, as Bacon relates, 'to carve windows into men's souls' – did not, however, diminish its traditional spirit of independence or its willingness to resist any encroachments on its rights. Norwich hated the Stuarts, for their improvidence and incompetence, and not least for the reckless determination of Charles I to impose upon them the High Church rituals and discipline of Archbishop Laud. In the city and the surrounding countryside, the religious reformers were strong, and the Puritans the natural leaders of society. Matthew Wren, whom Laud made bishop of Norwich, was an unsuitable choice by virtue of his character no less than his religious opinions: even the Earl of Clarendon, the Royalist historian of the Civil War, calls him 'a man of severe, sowr nature'. His persecution of Dissenters helps to explain why Norfolk, and Norwich in particular, so enthusiastically rallied to the Parliamentary cause. Like other Laudians, he was a patron of the arts, building the chapel of Pembroke College, Cambridge, which was designed for him

Sir Robert Walpole, who was given a triumphal welcome on his home ground, when he returned after his bitter defeat in Parliament.

by his famous nephew, Christopher. But what Norwich remembered was his abuse of the Church courts, which drove Protestants to leave not merely the city and district, but to emigrate to America; according to the articles of impeachment drawn up against Bishop Wren in 1641, his severity had forced three thousand people to leave the diocese – including the forebear of Abraham Lincoln. So Wren spent eighteen years in the Tower, emerging only at the Restoration; his cathedral was deserted, except when, on Guild-days, it served as quarters for the Mayor's guard of musketeers; and the city fathers attended, instead, the massive Perpendicular church of St Peter Mancroft, where they heard, among other sermons, one entitled: 'The Nail hit upon the Head and driven into the City and Cathedral Wall of Norwich.' Norwich became the centre of the powerful Eastern Association of Parliamentary forces, which formed the nucleus of the triumphant New Model Army, and thus the instrument of Cromwell's victories at home and abroad. The role the city played in the Civil War was thus in its tradition of resolute response to the abuse of authority.

Even in more settled and constitutional times, Norwich has tended to make up its own mind about public issues, irrespective of metropolitan opinion. In the eighteenth and nineteenth centuries, parliamentary managers always kept a very close watch on the Norfolk seats, which were more frequently contested than most, and could never be taken for granted. It is a fact that, even today, some Norfolk seats baffle psephologists by failing to reflect the national swings during general elections, and by defying the 'cube rule'. The city has always tended to cherish the great men who have sprung from the locality, even (perhaps more so) when they have fallen into national disfavour. After Sir Robert Walpole had been defeated in Parliament over his Excise Bill in 1733, he returned in some bitterness to his home ground in Norfolk, and was much cheered to be given a triumphal reception in Norwich. He, like Elizabeth, was put up in the Bishop's Palace, and the next day presented with a gold casket by the corporation. More than a thousand men greeted him and his brother three miles from the city, and gentry families escorted their coach. 'At eight in the evening they entered the city midst the loud exclamations of all sorts of people, the higher and lower gentry. The crowds were so great, that within the memory of man there were never so many people in the Market Place together, on any occasion whatsoever.'

Elections for the two Norfolk county seats – regarded as among the most valuable parliamentary prizes in the kingdom – were enormously expensive, for the electorate was exceptionally large by pre-Reform standards and voters had to come to Norwich for the polls and be kept entertained while the three-week polling lasted. The great county families, Whig and Tory, thus tried to avoid a contest by sharing the two seats, but whenever party feeling ran high, and compromise proved impossible, the money was poured out in thousands. In 1806, the Whigs, led by Thomas Coke, universally known as 'Coke of Norfolk' by virtue of his vast estates and agricultural experiments, tried to grab both seats for their party by putting up a minister, William Windham, as Coke's running-mate. The Tories rallied round Colonel John Wodehouse, who was their sole candidate: Tory voters could thus 'plump' for him, as it was called, by using only one of their two votes. Two of Wodehouse's grand female relatives, Mrs Berney and Mrs Atkins, infuriated the Whigs by campaigning for the Colonel with an enthusiasm which was judged unseemly. So the young Whigs dressed up two well-known Norwich prostitutes as the Tory ladies, hoisted them into a fine coach, and drew them in triumphant procession through the city. The Tory mob attacked, dragged the whores down and beat them, smashed the coach to bits and burnt the debris in the Market Place. Wodehouse was outraged at the insult offered to his womenfolk, and when he lost the election successfully petitioned for the verdict to be nullified. The affair cost all concerned a great deal of hard-earned Norfolk cash and was the talk of the nation and the delight of the city.

But Englishmen, at this time, were also talking of a more reputable aspect of the vigour and originality which Norwich could manifest. A London newspaper justly noted in 1823: 'The city of Norwich of late years has merited the approbation and applause of the metropolitan artists, from the number of landscape painters and draftsmen who have successfully studied the arts within its ancient walls.' The rise of the Norwich School was not an accident of history. The painting of landscape has been England's most significant and characteristic contribution to the visual arts, and watercolour the medium in which its artists have excelled all others. Now it is the wide but varied surfaces of East Anglia, and the enormous skies which overhang them, which offer the most satisfying challenge to the landscape artist; and it is watercolour, which forces the painter to work at great speed, blending subtlety with intense concentration, which best captures the fleeting moments of light and shade, the waxing and waning of colours, of an East Anglian panorama under sun and cloud. Turner, the internationalist and cosmopolitan, could draw inspiration wherever he travelled, and his burning appetite for colour drew him to the Mediterranean south, and the extremes of convulsed nature. But Constable, a much more typically English artist, returned always to his Suffolk horizons; and John Crome, the founder of the Norwich School, scarcely ever left Norfolk, or wished to paint elsewhere.

Crome, like nearly all the Norfolk artists, was born, schooled and bred in Norwich, the son of the keeper of the Griffin Inn. The only training he got was under a painter of coachwork and inn-signs; and he made his living by teaching art at the Grammar School, and by giving lessons to the daughters of the nearby gentry, travelling from house to house like a country doctor.

Opposite Coalbrookdale: the iron bridge – 'the first in the history of the world'.

John Gurney, the Quaker head of the famous Norwich banking firm of Gurney and Sons, gave him some patronage; otherwise, he does not seem to have received much financial support from the city he loved. His masterpiece, depicting Mousehold Heath, which is just outside Norwich, fetched only £25 and he was forced to teach his art six days a week, leaving only Sunday for his own work. But there was no doubt of the intensity of his attachment to his locale. In 1803, he and his artist brother-in-law, Robert Ladbrooke, founded the Norwich Society, 'An Inquiry into the Rise, Progress and Present State of Painting, Architecture, and Sculpture, with a view to pointing out the Best Methods of Study to attain to Greater Perfection in these Arts.' A few years later there were thirty-seven members, all active painters, mostly of watercolour landscapes. They included John Thirtle, James Stark, Henry Ninham, Joseph Stannard and the Reverend E. T. Daniell – all considerable artists, and most of them taught by Crome himself. In 1806 they were joined by John Sell Cotman, another of Crome's pupils, perhaps the most consummate water-colourist who has ever lived. Most of these artists spent their entire lives in Norwich, some dying in the houses where they were born. And they were humble folk. Cotman was the son of a Norwich hairdresser, Thirtle of a shoemaker. Henry Ninham, like Crome, came to the art through signpainting. Their paintings are overwhelmingly of Norfolk and Norwich scenes: the graceful old town, as it was in the early nineteenth century, springs to life in their pictures.

It is true that Cotman, conscious, perhaps, of his great powers, several times left Norwich to try his fortune in London. There, he was told by John Opie RA, in whose studio he worked for a time, 'Better black boots than follow the profession of an artist'. Opie said he was likely, despite his talent, to 'pine in indigence, or skulk through life as a drawing-master or pattern drawer to young ladies'. So, in a sense, it proved. At a Christie's sale in 1836 he saw his wonderful watercolour *Greta Bridge* knocked down for eight shillings, and he bought in his *Dismasted Brig* himself for seventeen shillings – both are now among the glories of the British Museum. He never made any kind of living from his crea-tive work, and supported his family by teaching – thus earning £150 a year – and by circulating six hundred of his drawings to lady-subscribers, who paid a guinea a quarter to copy them under his supervision: this helps to explain the huge number of forgeries which circulate under his name.

Cotman returned to Norwich to die; his red-brick Georgian house still stands in St Martin's-at-Palace Plain. Most of his artist-colleagues wisely kept to Norwich, even though it gave them only a modest patronage. There, they painted its streets and river, its wharves and bridges, and especially its churches – the same churches where, in most cases, they were baptized, married and buried. In this respect they followed Crome's sturdy local patriotism. Laurence Binyon, whose *John Crome and John Sell*

Above left John Cotman (1782–1842) and *above right* his teacher John Crome (1768–1821), the major artists of the Norwich School of painting.

Cotman (1897) first alerted modern taste to the importance of the school, wrote: 'Norwich was the only place which possessed artists of sufficient strength to create a rival centre to London, and the Norwich School would not have been possible had Crome left his native city for London, like every other genius of the provinces.' As it was, these Norwich painters were at their best when they worked in their own county: even Cotman's art suffered when, in London, he used the new, brilliant colours which could only be bought in the metropolis, and the expensive, non-absorbent cartridge paper made by Messrs Whatman's. His pictures which we now prize the most are soft, subdued, reticent, almost Japanese in their subtle but limited range of colours, and in their formal arrangements of line and mass. They reflect the atmosphere, lights and tints of Norfolk, and they were created from materials which Crome had taught him, and his Norwich contemporaries, to mix and use.

As it happened, not long after Crome died, he received a splendid tribute from another Norfolk man, that great eccentric George Borrow, who had been taught by Crome at Norwich Grammar School. Borrow heard that his brother, a would-be artist, was proposing to leave Norwich and study in Italy, and he addressed to him a notable letter which he reproduced in his autobiographical novel, *Lavengro*:

Seekest thou inspiration? Thou needst it not: thou hast it already; and it was never yet found by crossing the sea . . . To Gainsborough and Hogarth turn, not names of the world, maybe, but English names – and England against the world! A living master? Why, there he comes, thou hast had him long, he has long guided thy young hand towards the excellence which is yet far from thee, but which thou canst attain if thou shouldst persist and wrestle, even as he has done, amid gloom and despondency . . . he who now comes up the little creaking stairs to thy little studio in the second floor to inspect thy last effort before thou departest; the little stout man whose face is very dark, and whose eye is vivacious; that man has attained excellence, destined some day to be acknowledged, though not till he is cold, and his mortal part returned to its kindred clay. He has painted, not pictures of the world, but English pictures, such as Gainsborough himself might have done; beautiful rural pieces, with trees which might well tempt the little birds to perch upon them . . . the little dark man with the brown coat and the top-boots, whose name will one day be considered the chief ornament of the old town, and whose works will at no distant period rank among the proudest pictures in England – and England against the world! – thy master, my brother, thy, at present, all too little considered master – Crome!

What Borrow's rhetoric failed to establish – the majestic place of Crome, Cotman and their city-colleagues in the history of British art – was later brought about by James Reeve, the indefatigable curator of the Norwich Museum, who spent his entire professional life assembling a huge collection of their drawings, paintings, letters and documents. It is on the basis of this collection that modern scholarly appreciation of the school rests. Much of the material Reeve gathered is in the British Museum. But there is a fine collection, too, in Norwich itself, now housed in the stately castle keep, so surprisingly and lovingly decorated by the Norman garrison eight centuries ago. So, at Norwich, the visitor can both delight in the ancient town itself, scarred but still triumphantly surviving the ravages of progress, and examine it as it appeared to the gifted eyes of England's greatest school of provincial painters. Norwich, in fact, has everything an English cathedral city should have, not least a superb visual record of its past, before the Juggernauts came.

9 GREENWICH

'Down to the sea in ships'

Left above The Queen's House, Greenwich: designed originally by Inigo Jones, it was completed by John Webb.

Below The Royal Institution: Faraday at work in his laboratory.

THERE IS NO DOUBT that the best way to approach Greenwich is by water, and preferably from downstream. There comes a point, as your boat rounds the man-made headland formed by the London Underground's power-station, when the finest architectural panorama in England – some would say in Europe – springs into view. The stone steps of the Royal Naval College dip into the water. On either side, its massive stone façades draw the eye irresistibly to the two baroque domes which crown each wing; these, in turn, frame the elegant double-cube of the Queen's House; and the roof of the House is a platform from which the eye moves up the green slopes of Greenwich Park, to the angular, red-brick silhouette of the Restoration Royal Observatory, which completes the vista. Water and grass, stone and brick: these elements were blended together over more than a century by five of England's greatest architects, Inigo Jones, John Webb, his son-in law, Sir Christopher Wren, Nicholas Hawksmoor and Sir John Vanbrugh – and they form a stage on which a good deal of English history has been enacted.

Indeed, the stage was there long before the present composition took shape. It was Humphrey, Duke of Gloucester, youngest brother of Henry V, who first picked on Greenwich as the site for a palace, in 1428. He called it 'Bella Vista', a name not yet degraded by suburban familiarity, and there he housed the rich collection of books and manuscripts which later became the nucleus of the Bodleian Library, Oxford. Margaret of Anjou, the ferocious wife of his nephew, Henry VI, took it over and enlarged it; and, when Henry VII terminated the Wars of Roses at Bosworth, he embellished it with brick and stone pinnacles, making it his chief palace on the lower reaches of the Thames. Henry VIII was born at Greenwich, as was his daughter Elizabeth; her mother, Anne Boleyn, was arrested there, and taken upstream to the Tower for mock-trial and execution. Henry VIII built an armoury at Greenwich, and naval yards at nearby Woolwich and Deptford; and in Elizabeth's day the palace was the display-centre for England's naval and military might, where ambassa-

The Royal College, Greenwich, seen from the Isle of Dogs – the 'finest architectural panorama in England – some would say in Europe'.

dors came to be impressed. From the river-gatehouse she watched her fleet exercise, and from the park-gatehouse, at the rear, she reviewed her troops: 'guns were discharged on one another, the morris-pikes encountered together with great alarm; each ran to their weapons again, and then they fell together as fast as they could, in imitation of close combat' (1559). Once, leaving Greenwich by barge, she was nearly killed by a careless wildfowler, who discharged his piece accidentally and sent a bullet through the arm of one of the royal oarsmen; the offender was taken to the steps to be hanged, but pardoned as the rope was placed round his neck. In the banqueting-hall, Holbein's first royal commission, five hundred guests dined on occasion; and in the chapel, a delighted Danish ambassador heard the Office 'so melodiously sung and said . . . as a man half-dead might thereby have been quickened'.

James I, a homosexual who preferred to keep his wife, the pathetic Anne of Denmark, in separate quarters, asked Inigo Jones, in 1616, to build her a house behind the Old Palace. He produced England's first truly Palladian design: a square, sparse and elegant box, simplicity itself without, gorgeous within; it must have struck contemporaries as devastatingly 'modern'. Anne died before the house was finished; and, though work was resumed for her daughter-in-law, Henrietta Maria, the building-process was overtaken by the Civil War. The War was fatal for Old Greenwich, as it was for so many other splendid royal palaces. Parliament maintained Whitehall and Hampton Court, the rest

146

were allowed to decay. Greenwich became an army biscuit factory, then a prison for Dutch captives, and when Charles II got his throne back he found he had no alternative but to pull the old Tudor buildings down. The Queen's House remained, and was at last completed by John Webb, who had married the designer's daughter. But it was never a real home for royalty: it became a perk of the Ranger of Greenwich Park, then a home for distinguished naval men, and a school for the children of poor seamen; finally, in 1937, the navy transformed it into the National Maritime Museum, which now houses the most magnificent and comprehensive collection of maritime objects in the world, from the uniform Nelson wore at Trafalgar to the *Reliant*, the world's last steam-paddle vessel, preserved intact.

Meanwhile, what was to be done with the site of the Old Palace? In Elizabethan times, the state made no provision for the seamen on which its security rested. They were taken off the payroll as soon as danger receded, and turned loose on the streets. Some were graciously issued with licences to beg, and parliament commanded parishes to hold collections. In 1590, John Hawkins, the warmest-hearted of Elizabeth's sea-dogs, who had already endowed (from the profits of slave-trading) an almshouse for ten 'decayed mariners', set up the 'Chatham Chest' to provide doles for his old shipmates. It was, literally, an iron-bound chest; the one which survives dating from the early seventeenth century and now in the Museum, had five locks, the keys to which were held by five officers, to prevent peculation. But the provision was grievously inadequate. After the Restoration, the diarist John Evelyn produced a scheme to build a Royal Hospital, or alms-house for sailors, on the site of Greenwich Old Palace. Charles II was keen to develop Greenwich as a centre of naval lore and display. On the hill he set up an observatory, in which the first Astronomer Royal lived, beneath a great observation platform designed by Wren and his colleagues in the Office of Works. But Charles had no money for a hospital, or indeed to pay his sailors while they were still in his service. In 1665, Samuel Pepys, the naval secretary, was in Greenwich to see the fleet discharged. He reported that the Naval Office was 'assailed all day by the horrible crowd and lamentable moan of the poor seamen that lie starving . . . for lack of money'. 'The whole [ship's] company of the *Breda*,' he wrote, 'are now breaking the windows of our office, swearing they will not budge without money. What meat they'll make of me anon, you shall hear by my next.'

So Evelyn's scheme languished, to be resurrected in the patriotic aftermath of the great naval victory at La Hogue in 1692. Then, as the Latin inscription on the frieze of the great hall records, 'The pious regard of Queen Mary dedicated this Palace of Greenwich for the relief and maintenance, at the public expense, of those seamen who have protected the public safety in the reign of William and Mary, 1694.' 'Public expense' in fact meant 'private subscription', and although grandees like the King and the Archbishop of Canterbury led the list with large sums, Evelyn, appointed Treasurer of the commission, often found it hard to collect the cash. Nevertheless, the commission's work went forward, with Wren one of its members and Vanbrugh the secretary. On 30 June 1696, a delighted Evelyn recorded: 'Went with a select committee of the Commissioners for Greenwich Hospital, and with Sir Christopher Wren, where with him I laid

The ancient Palace of Placentia, from One Tree Hill, *c.* 1620 (detail, anon).

the first stone of the intended foundation, precisely at 5 o'clock in the evening, after we had dined together, Mr Flamsteed, the King's astronomical professor, observing the punctual time by instruments.' Evelyn was present again nearly a decade later, in 1705, when the first seamen were admitted: 'The buildings now going on are very magnificent.' Indeed they were, and are. Though like most great English architectural conceptions, it was never quite completed according to the original plan, and though Vanbrugh, Hawksmoor and others from the Office of Work made their contribution, it is nevertheless essentially the Baroque palace as Wren conceived it. The connection between its spacious stone halls and chambers, and the relief of poor seamen, is not visually obvious; indeed, Dr Johnson, on visiting it, made the practical point: 'It is too magnificent for a place of charity.' But Wren was not thinking in prosaic terms. The Hospital was to be the triumph of his art on the South Bank, as is St Paul's on the North; and so it is.

As a home for old seamen, the Hospital lasted 150 years. Its swelling funds were augmented, in 1803, by amalgamation with the Chatham Chest, and as a result a new range of buildings was added, so that by 1815 the inmates had reached their maximum number of 2,710. Out-pensions were also awarded, to officers and men and, in theory, every man in the Navy and Marines could claim a pension, or a place in the Hospital, though he had to qualify under very intricate rules. In practice, recommendations by senior (or influential) officers were needed to win a place. The pensioners lived in 'wards', as in therapeutic hospitals, got their board and lodging free, and a shilling a week pocket-money. Each ward was in the charge of an elected Boatswain, who got half-a-crown, and his two 'Mates', paid 6d extra. From the 1740s, when the active navy was put into uniform, the inmates were issued with blue tailcoats and breeches, cocked hats and blue stockings (the Boatswain and his Mates had gold stripes on their coats). Nightgowns, neckerchiefs and bedding were also provided, and greatcoats for the elderly. Discipline was strict, offenders being put into yellow coats with red sleeves until they were pardoned. But morale was high, for the men were well treated, and many indeed lived to a great age. In 1803, ninety-six of the pensioners were over eighty, sixteen over ninety, and one over a hundred; one batch of a hundred men averaged eighty-two years, six months apiece, with twenty-five years service under the mast; six of them had served for over fifty years. Greenwich, in the eighteenth and early nineteenth centuries was a living, as well as a monumental showpiece, appearing to testify to the munificence of the English state, and the care it bestowed on former servants.

Therein lay an anomaly, for the comfort of the Hospital was in flagrant contrast to the manner in which the sailors were treated during their active days. They were underpaid, underfed, over-punished and, in effect, deprived of their civil rights. From the time of Cromwell until 1797, their basic wage remained unchanged: 19s a month, less than half that of a merchant seaman. In that year it was raised by 6s 6d, but the highest rate a lower-deck man could reach was £3 1s a month, less than a tenth of the salary paid to the captain of a first-rate. Moreover, officers benefited from a complex system of 'allowances', the right to carry and import certain quantities of goods freight and duty-free, and above all from prize-money (of which, it is true, the men got a tiny share). Prizes made many flag-officers and captains rich men: during the Napoleonic Wars half-a-dozen saved over £200,000 each, and £50,000 was not uncommon. A four-year spell as Commander-in-Chief in the West Indies was calculated to be worth £100,000. By contrast, most seamen left the navy penniless.

What made matters worse was the system by which the men were recruited in the first place. It is a popular fallacy that conscription was unknown in England until the First World War. Englishmen had always been under a legal obligation to serve their country in wartime, though service was exacted from them in an arbitrary manner. The land-militia was augmented by compulsory ballot, from which a man could exempt himself by paying a substitute to serve in his place. Merchant seamen, legally defined as 'persons using the sea', were excused the ballot but were subject to impressment. Some volunteered, for successful captains with a good record for taking prizes could attract the adventurous, as recruiting posters preserved in the Museum testify. But most seamen naturally preferred the better pay and conditions of the merchant marine, and it was these, chiefly, who were 'pressed'. The press was hedged by legal restrictions. Strictly speaking, it could only press experienced seamen, and those only from homeward bound ships or discharged crews; masters, pilots, ship's carpenters and a host of others, including 'those with the appearance of a gentleman', were likewise exempt. When the navy was challenged in the courts over an illegal impressment, it almost always released the man rather than fight the case. But with the enormous expansion of the navy during the Napoleonic Wars – 600,000 men, all told, served on the lower deck – the rules were increasingly flouted, especially when a national Impress Service replaced the efforts of individual captains. The press operated everywhere, and landsmen, colonials, foreigners, even enemies, were drawn into the net. In 1808, the *Implacable*'s complement of 563 included sixteen West Indies blacks, fifteen Scandinavians, eleven Germans, twenty-eight Americans, and others from all over the world. At least seventy-one foreigners, including Frenchmen, served on the *Victory* at Trafalgar (it should be added that Villeneuve's flagship included fifteen Britons, all deserters). Foreigners were seized, as needed, whenever a king's ship touched port, the press being sent out the night before the ship weighed anchor, to prevent interference from consuls: such arbitrary behaviour was one principal cause

Opposite A Navy recruiting poster of the 1790s.

THREE MEN FOR THE
NAVY.

WANTED

For the Townships of Chipping, Dutton,

And Clayton-le-Dale,

THREE ABLE-BODIED
Seamen or Landmen,

TO ferve in his Majefty's NAVY during the prefent War only; and as the Time for accepting fuch Volunteers expires on *Wednefday* next, the 14th of *December*, it is hoped that no True-Born BRITISH TAR will lofe fo favourable an Opportunity. Such as make an immediate Application will be preferred, and over and above a handfome Bounty, will be entitled to, and receive, Advantages fuperior to any other Service, viz. The Families and Friends of Volunteers will receive Monthly Pay, and the Volunteers themfelves will have a bountiful Supply of CLOATHING, BEEF, GROG, FLIP, and STRONG BEER, alfo a Certainty of PRIZE-MONEY, as the Men entered for this Service will be fent to Capture

The Rich Spanifh Galleons,

and in Confequence will return loaded with DOLLARS and HONOURS, to fpend their Days in PEACE and PLENTY.
HUZZA!!!

☞ BOUNTY will be paid by applying to JOHN SWINGLEHURST, of *Chipping*; THOMAS DEWHURST, of *Dutton*; and JAMES HIGGS, of *Clayton-le-Dale*.

BLACKBURN: J. WATERWORTH, PRINTER.

A panorama of the Royal
Hospital of Greenwich,
c. 1725.

of the Anglo-American war of 1812. In 1795 Pitt introduced a new
form of conscription, the 'Quota', under which the counties were
obliged to supply specified numbers of men for naval service.
Naturally, they turned out the inmates of their gaols, as they had
been doing for army service since the Middle Ages, and it was the
'Quota Men' who formed the ringleaders of the great mutinies
in 1797.

The bulk of the fleet – more than fifty per cent in fact – was
manned by the press, however; and these sailors were denied
shore-leave in home ports. They had to serve until the end of
hostilities, unless they could buy themselves out, which meant
saving £11 – a year's pay. Many were released only by death.
Battle was the least they had to fear; in the whole of the Seven
Years' War the navy lost only 1,512 men killed in action, against
133,708 who deserted or died of disease and accident. Nelson
lost 895 men at the Nile, 941 at Copenhagen, 1,690 at Trafalgar.
Most men died from scurvy, which, for instance, cost George
Anson 626 men out of a complement of 961 during his world
cruise of 1740–4, or from infectious disease. It was the old tale:
defeating the Armada cost the lives of a mere hundred English
seamen, but 10,000 died of sickness in the weeks that followed.
Shipwreck, too, took a heavy toll. Throughout the Napoleonic
Wars, the navy lost only ten ships by enemy action, but eighty-
four were wrecked, chiefly during the long years of inshore, all-
weather, all-season blockade of the French coast. The pressed
seaman, as Dr Johnson remarked, was worse off than in gaol, for

he had lost his freedom, and his life in addition was in near-continuous peril. Whenever possible, he deserted: over 12,000 did so successfully in the two-year period leading up to Trafalgar.

But for some of the survivors, at least, there was the safe refuge of Greenwich. It even had its strictly medical staff: a physician, a surgeon, a dispenser (or apothecary), six assistants and four matrons. Thus it supplemented the navy's own system of hospitals for the sick, which included two major establishments at Haslar and Plymouth and 'sick quarters' at a score of British ports and nine overseas stations. Like civilian hospitals, they killed more than they cured. George Watson, a Nelsonian sailor who published a revealing account of his life in 1827, *Adventures of a Greenwich Pensioner*, claimed: 'The nurses . . . were chiefly of the frail sisterhood . . . exceedingly bold and audacious, and without concern they make use of the most indecent observations and actions in their common conversation. I had a great deal to do to repulse the temptations I met with from these Syrens.' But the age to which most Greenwich pensioners lived suggests that the navy acted as a survival-of-the-fittest process; the weak died, the strong flourished.

The chief complaint was the absence of women. Married pensioners were not allowed to bring their wives into the Hospital. Greenwich girls, especially its army of fisherwomen, were

Below Tars Carousing by George Cruikshank. Women were sometimes hidden aboard warships on active service: a dozen were present at the Battle of the Nile.

notorious. Pepys, in 1665, had called the place 'the greatest nursery of lewd women, beggars and bastards about the City'. But doubtless the pensioners smuggled in females, as they had learned to do at sea. Women were allowed on naval vessels in port, and sometimes on voyage between home ports, but never, in theory, on active service. In fact, there is abundant evidence that the men got them on board, and kept them in the darker recesses of the ships. There was at least one woman, Jane Townshend, present at Trafalgar on the *Defiance*; and she later made good her claim to the General Service Medal (though the Navy meanly refused to issue it to her). Perhaps a dozen women were present at the Battle of the Nile, and some of them were wounded; one gave birth to a child during the action. Some of those listed in ships' companies as 'boys' and 'ratings' were undoubtedly women; and it emerged in 1815 that a pretty black girl had served as an Able Seaman on the *Queen Charlotte* for no less than eleven years! There was more to the unreformed navy than, to quote Churchill's famous phrase, 'rum, buggery and the lash'.

If Greenwich was a safe haven for old ABs, it also offered comfortable billets for well-connected gentlemen. The Governor, always an Admiral, lived in splendour in the Queen's House, and many other serving and former officers were comfortably lodged on the property, with substantial stipends. In 1830, when the Whigs got back to power, that delightful letter writer, Thomas Creevey, was rewarded for past political services by being given the office (now a sinecure) of Treasurer of Greenwich Hospital. The post had a salary of £600 a year, and carried with it a splendid house in Old School Lane, free of taxes, with coal and candles supplied, bread at the low official contract prices, and as many pensioners as he liked for servants, paid 6d a day – altogether, Creevey exulted, 'worth a good thousand a year'. In return, he attended board-meetings (the real accountancy was done by clerks). The beauty of it all, he wrote, was that the Hospital was financed by its endowments, and was thus immune to the new forces of reform: 'Thank God we are all out of reach of Parliament. We live upon our own, without a stiver of public money to be voted for us by that infernal House of Commons.'

Indeed, the long years of peace which followed the Congress of Vienna were the great days of the Hospital. Greenwich had its own little society of naval officers, contractors, civilian officials, and the gentry who built villas around the park and on the salubrious heights of nearby Blackheath. Creevey had his personal pew in the Chapel for Sunday service, and went to numerous local entertainments. In fact it was Greenwich society which eventually killed him. On 2 February 1838, he 'stayed over long at Greenwich' gossiping with the daughters of the Governor, Admiral Sir Thomas Hardy, who had been Nelson's flag-captain at Trafalgar; caught cold in the night air, and died. Often, Greenwich society was augmented when great naval feasts took

An old view of the famous *Ship Tavern* at Greenwich which still stands today.

place in the Hall, under the tremendous Baroque ceiling painted by Sir James Thornhill – feasts which were precursors of the Trafalgar Dinners which the navy still holds there on the anniversary of the battle. Then, too, the place was famous for its fresh fish, magnificently served by five well-found inns. The grandees of Westminster, Whitehall and the City, came there for uproarious fish-dinners, travelling down river in elaborate painted barges, some of which can still be seen in the Museum. This was the custom of the cabinet, on the night Parliament went into recess, as Charles Greville records: 'At the end of the season there is always a fish-dinner at Greenwich, the whipper-in [chief whip] Ben Stanley in the chair . . . everybody saying what he pleases, and dealing out gibes and jests upon his friends.' It was a place for out-of-town unbuttoning, and Lord Brougham, the Lord Chancellor, continued to go there to celebrate, with society ladies, long after he left the cabinet; as did famous novelists, like Dickens and Thackeray, as well as thousands of more obscure Londoners – 'cits', as Mr Jorrocks called them.

But with the arrival of Victorian prosperity, the number of naval pensioners began to fall. Sailors were better paid, and encouraged to save; after 1849, there were more places available to in-pensioners than applicants ready to fill them, and by 1865 only 1,400 were left in the Hospital. Four years later, the pensioners were given the option of a capital sum, and the great majority took it; the rest were transferred to other institutions, and the Hospital, as such, disestablished. But the English are ingenious at discovering new uses for ancient foundations which have outlived their purpose, and in 1873 the navy refurbished the Hospital to serve as its professional training college.

Considering the high element of technology and expertise

Pensioners dining at Greenwich Hospital in 1865. Victorian prosperity meant that their numbers were declining by this time.

which had always been required in directing the royal ships, the navy had been extraordinarily slow in making provision for the standardized training of officers. All was left to individual captains. Once the captain had received his commission to proceed to sea on active service, the composition of its crew, officers and men, was largely his own choice. It is true that only the Crown could provide the commission which made an officer; but as the candidates sent to the Admiralty for selection were appointed by captains, in practice they determined who were commissioned. In 1676 the ingenious Pepys had invented a system whereby

young men were nominated by the Admiralty for shipboard training as future officers, and a generation later in 1733, an academy was set up in Portsmouth to instruct forty such pupils, 'the sons of the Nobility and Gentry'. It languished, and in 1801, Lord St Vincent, the Admiralty organizer of Nelson's victories, dismissed it as 'a sink of vice and abomination'. It was modernized five years later, under the leading expert in ship-construction, maths and gunnery, James Inman; even so, it turned out less than two-and-a-half per cent of the navy's officers, and of every forty officers appointed to the fleet, thirty-nine owed their advancement to captains. Many joined ship at the age of nine and, by presenting fake birth-certificates, got their lieutenant's commission at sixteen. Promotion, too, was arranged by 'influence', at least as high as post-captain, after which seniority became the determining factor. Senior officers, Ministers, Members of Parliament – anyone who was in a position to render a favour to, or extract one from, the Admiralty – operated the influence system. It is true that the navy, unlike the army, avoided cash payments; a man could not 'buy' a ship, in the way he could buy a regiment, or a rank, which became a negotiable freehold; and the navy was notably less aristocratic, more than fifty per cent of its officers coming from professional families. But even the greatest commanders, like Nelson and Collingwood, both benefited from and used 'influence'; St Vincent was, perhaps, the only famous exception.

The coming of steam and ironclads, and the revolutionary technology both involved, forced a change in the methods of training officers. In 1873 the Royal Naval College was refounded at Greenwich, and lieutenants who had been trained as midshipmen on such ships as the *Britannia* were obliged to take a triple course in navigation, gunnery and general studies. But the atmosphere of the College was conservative, as was the Admiralty, which determined its curriculum. In the decade before the First World War, the navy declined, despite Churchill's efforts, to set up a general staff (like the army), or to draw up detailed contingency plans for war. Hence in 1914, it was the army which shaped the general course of British strategy, with lamentable results; and the navy, by delaying the adoption of the convoy system, nearly lost us the war. Here is another case of a British institution which has produced brilliant innovating individuals but, as a corporate entity, has resisted necessary change.

Today, the navy finds itself increasingly the custodian of Britain's strategic deterrent, through its nuclear-powered missile-carrying submarines. The Naval College reflects this responsibility, with its top-secret nuclear training establishment. The casual visitor will see little evidence of the modern navy, however; its mysteries, horrific or arcane, are concealed behind Wren's stone walls, and the Senior Service remains a silent one. Ostensibly, at least, Greenwich is a monument to the past, and a past dominated by sail. In a dry dock near the College is the 1870s

PRIME MERIDIAN
OF THE WORLD

Above right Children playing on the meridian line at the Old Royal Observatory.

Left The Cutty Sark, once the fastest tea-clipper on the seas, and now preserved in dry dock.

tea-clipper *Cutty Sark*, rescued from oblivion, refitted from stem to stern and open to the public since 1957; all made possible by public subscription (like the Royal Hospital itself). She has since been joined, on the nearby quay, by *Gipsy Moth IV*, in which Sir Francis Chichester became the first man to circumnavigate the world single-handed. On the hill, Charles II's observatory has become a museum, for pollution has not driven the Observatory Royal itself to the clearer air of Herstmonceaux in Sussex. Here can be seen, not the instruments of modern astro-physics, but the quadrants and astrolabes, the polyhedral sundials, the equin-octial ring-dials, the maps, globes, compasses, sectors and tele-scopes which Flamsteed and his contemporaries used. Within the security perimeter, Greenwich holds secrets of life and death. But to the tourist it is, rather, a window into the past, a past embracing five hundred years of British and world maritime history, and rich with the triumphs, disasters, anomalies, suffer-ings, customs and glamour of a great fighting service.

Ironbridge today, the
'cradle of an entirely new
civilization, at least as
important in its contribution
to man's progress as Babylon
or Alexandria, Athens or
Rome'.

10 IRONBRIDGE
Cradle of the Modern World

IT IS AN ARGUABLE proposition that the Industrial Revolution was the great watershed in human history, the point at which mankind first began to establish a real mastery over his environment. If this be conceded, then Coalbrookdale has some claims to be considered the cradle of an entirely new civilization, at least as important in its contribution to man's progress as Babylon or Alexandria, Athens or Rome. Almost as though it were conscious of its historic claims, the place has acquired, over the last century, a venerable air. Industry is now silent: industrial archaeology has taken its place. In Shropshire, where the Coalbrook joins the Severn, the waters pass through a gorge for a quarter of a mile, the valley sides falling from four hundred to fifty feet. The valley, with its woods and cliffs, must have been beautiful before industry came; now it is so again, but with a different kind of beauty, the ruined engines and mills, forges and foundries, abandoned like broken toys, constituting a poignant and even poetic comment on man's insatiable appetite for wealth and power. It is already a museum, preserved as such in fact, with its centrepiece the triumphant iron bridge – the first in the history of the world – which spans the gorge. Increasingly, men and women will come here to conjure up the past, as they have for generations visited the Pyramids, the Parthenon and the Forum.

Britain's Industrial Revolution, the prelude to all others, became a visible and unmistakable phenomenon in the 1770s and 1780s. But it had deep roots in the past. Indeed, in a sense one can trace its distant origins in the Iron Age. Since man first learned to use tools, the species has always dug in the earth to find durable materials which could be fashioned into implements. Once he discovered the properties of iron-ore, and how to turn it into solid and malleable metal by a simple charcoal furnace worked by wind – what was later to be called a 'bloom' – the only problem was how to manufacture enough of it. Societies rose by their capacity to produce iron instruments for farming and war in sufficient quantities; it was the basic criterion of progress and power. The problem revolved around the type of fuel used: wood was in limited supply, and there were many other demands on it. Coal was known to be available as a fuel, and had in fact been used in very small quantities since Roman times. But how could coal be used to produce iron? – there was the baffling dilemma.

The Shropshire hills have produced coal and iron-ore throughout recorded history. Indeed it has been established that the Romans mined coal at Oakengates to fuel their hypocausts. Whether they made iron there is conjectural: the Ordnance Survey *Map of Roman Britain* lists no such site, and their main source of supply was much farther south, in the Forest of Dean. In the Middle Ages, English iron was produced chiefly in the Weald, where the supply of timber for charcoal was abundant. But in Shropshire some iron-ore deposits were worked and coal was mined in growing quantities. The earliest surviving licence to dig for coal in Shropshire dates from about 1260. At Benthall coal was produced from at least 1326; and four years earlier, Walter de Caldebrook was licensed by Wenlock Priory to mine coal in the Severn Valley, near the place where the Ironbridge now stands. At Deer Leap, near Benthall, nineteenth-century miners found evidence of very ancient workings – wooden shovels, and flanged wooden wheels cut out of solid blocks, even an iron axel-tree: the remains, in fact, of Medieval wagons built to carry considerable weights. At Oakengates, in the oldest levels, they discovered some very primitive implements – wicker baskets, wooden spades cased in iron, and rush-wicked candles. These mining, and smelting, activities were carried out over a wide area, but on a very small scale, and chiefly in places where the ore and coal were near the surface. Visiting the Clee Hills in the early sixteenth century, the geographer and antiquary John Leland says: 'There be "blow-shops" on these hills.' The blow-shops were the bloom-furnaces, rudimentary affairs, consisting of little more than a pile of stones, arranged to get the full force of the wind. There was no casting: the pigs of iron were re-heated and hammered into shape in blacksmiths' shops. These wind-furnaces usually had to be sited high up in the hills, sometimes above the 1,700 contour; and the problem of transporting the metal limited production.

The Elizabethan age saw a steady expansion in mining and manufacturing. This was the deliberate policy of the government – to promote industry and make England self-sufficient, above all in war-materials, to stop the outflow of gold and reduce what we would now call the 'trade-gap'. The impulse to invest, particularly in mining, was enormously strengthened by the Dissolution of the Monasteries, and the reduction of episcopal estates. The clergy had been very conservative landlords, had usually declined to work minerals for themselves, and often flatly refused to issue licences to others. When Elizabeth curbed the palatine powers of the bishopric of Durham, and issued licences herself, there was a vast and rapid expansion of the Newcastle coalfield – the first to be exploited on a mass scale, for the seams were relatively near the sea, from which it could be cheaply shipped to London. Under Elizabeth, annual shipments of coal from Newcastle doubled every fifteen years; in the year 1581–2, one colliery alone produced 20,000 tons. England became a major exporter of coal: in the year 1594, 852 ships carried 35,934 tons of coal from Newcastle to foreign ports, and by the eve of the Civil War England was producing between three and four times as much coal as the entire Continent.

Geographically, Shropshire was less well placed than County Durham to exploit its coal resources. But then it had iron-ore, which Durham did not; and iron machinery was in growing demand to raise the output from the Newcastle pits. The Elizabethan nobility and gentry, most of them comparatively 'new' men, were enterprising and vigorous in their search for mineral and industrial sources of wealth. When they got possession of Church lands, they often seized eagerly on the opportunities their clerical predecessors had neglected. Thus the Sidney family began to mine and forge iron in Sussex the moment they were granted Robertsbridge Priory: it was producing two hundred tons a year by 1562. It was the Sidneys who established a connection between the Weald and the primitive Shropshire ironfield. For Sir Henry Sidney spent most of his career presiding over the Council of the Welsh Marches, which included Shropshire in its jurisdiction. He was so keen to produce a hard variety of iron, or steel, that he recruited workers from Germany, with two expert ironmasters to command them. The first proper blast-furnaces in Shropshire date from this time, erected with Sidney's encouragement. Other gentry also played their part. The Brookes of Madeley Court, a fine Elizabethan house now overshadowed by the new town of Telford, were keen entrepreneurs. The garden at Madeley testifies to their scientific interests, for it contains an ingenious astronomical toy, four feet square, which once rested on huge stone pillars. On the estate, in 1638, Sir Basil Brooke built what was later to be known as the 'Old Furnace' for iron-smelting; and it was at Madeley that James Foster, a century later, was to install the second steam engine ever built, to produce pig-iron (it is now in the South Kensington Science Museum). Madeley also supplied the Commonwealth forces with one of their leading commanders, for James Berry, a clerk at the iron-works, became captain of Cromwell's personal troop of horse, and was subsequently appointed Major-General in charge of Wales and Herefordshire. This was an early example of the association between the new industries and political radicalism – a process which was to culminate in the Great Reform Bill and the Repeal of the Corn Laws.

The Commonwealth evidently regarded Shropshire as a strategic area by virtue of its raw materials and forges. Shrewsbury itself was a centre of Royalist power, so a Parliamentary garrison was established at Benthall 'to prevent the enemy from gathering contributions in their county, and to stop coals from coming thither, and to Worcester, for at this place the coles [sic] that supplied those places are digged'. More and more coal mines were being opened up and at deeper and deeper levels; there was an increasing tendency, too, to differentiate between the various qualities and types of coal, which had now acquired their special names: Doubles, Tops, Deeps, Yard, Sulphur, Foot, Two-feet, Flints and Little Flints, Fungus, Clod and Guv. Shropshire Fungus, for instance, was regarded in London as the best coal.

But no one had yet successfully brought the two vital raw materials into conjunction by using coal to produce iron. Many Elizabethans had attempted to do so, as the issues of patents testify. In 1618, indeed, one of the Dudley family produced a coal-smelter, but he could not persuade the ironmasters that it was economically viable, and the invention died with him. Then, in 1708, a Quaker called Abraham Darby took a mineral lease at Coalbrookdale, having taken out a patent for 'a new way of casting'. He had been born near Dudley in 1676, the son and grandson of locksmiths, and around the turn of the century he was running a Bristol brassworks. He seems to have been a good man of business as well as an innovator. With his lease, he took over Sir Basil Brooke's Old Furnace and installed new equipment for coking coal. We do not know what was his precise process, but evidently the reconstructed furnace was quite small, worked by a bellows powered by water, and feeding the molten iron direct into the castings. He produced cast-iron successfully by this method at least as early as 1713; but other masters were very slow to follow his example, and it was not until 1745 that the Royal Society, in the person of the Reverend Mr Mason, reported that the new method was viable.

Abraham Darby died in 1717, leaving young sons, and the Coalbrookdale Company was created to manage the family business. It remained, for over a century, a closely-knit domestic concern, the sons and grandsons taking over the company as soon as they were old enough to do so, the daughters and grand-daughters, in the meantime, being married to men skilled in the trade, all Quakers. At first, the works produced comparatively simple products – iron pots, kettles, skillets, weights and 'garden rowles'. But in 1698, Thomas Newcomen, a Dartmouth black-smith, had made a stream-engine, fuelled by coal, and from 1712 this was successfully adapted for use in the coal-pits, where it pumped out water in the levels liable to flooding. This machine enormously increased the productivity and output of the pits and thus cut the cost of coal for iron-smelting; equally important, it created a demand for machinery, and it was this new demand that the Coalbrookdale Company proceeded to meet. It was producing 'Fire-Engines', as they were called, in the 1720s; and in the 1740s Abraham Darby II installed a large new engine to work his blast-furnace. Thus the works became an industrial matrix, designing and manufacturing its own machinery to produce machines for sale. In 1750 a further link in the chain was forged, when the

A coal miner with James Watt's steam-engine in the background. Watt worked closely with the industrial pioneers of Coalbrookdale.

works laid down a railway for its wagons: the rails made on the spot, were of wood, $3\frac{1}{2}$ inches by $4\frac{1}{2}$ inches, resting on wooden sleepers; the wagon-wheels, of iron, were cast in the foundry.

Abraham Darby II died in 1763, when the company was taken over by a local ironmaster, Richard Reynolds, who had married his eldest daughter. He, too, was an innovator: in 1768 he began to cast iron rails for the firm's railway. Initially, his object was simply to expand the track and enable it to carry heavier wagons – Shropshire roads were described as 'narrow, steep, unprotected, unfenced and almost impassable in winter'. But an iron railway offered dramatic opportunities for expanding mining and industry elsewhere, especially in the Newcastle coalfield, and this new market led to further development of the Coalbrookdale works. The process of industrialization was thus reaching the crucial point modern economists call 'take-off', in which expansion becomes self-generating, almost irresistible: inventions are developed to solve problems and in doing so create new demands which require more inventions to fulfil them, and so on in an endless cycle of progress. When the patent of James Watt's improved steam-engine was confirmed by Parliament in 1775, the Coalbrookdale works was completely re-equipped, Watt being paid one-third of the saving in coal. Watt's engine was vastly more efficient than anything produced hitherto and its range of uses constantly expanding; it was already evident that, sooner or later, steam power could be used for transit as well as static propulsion: thus it fitted into the situation created by the manufacture of iron rails like the missing piece in a jigsaw. Indeed, it is as a jigsaw that we should see the process by which the Industrial Revolution got under way; slowly the pieces were fitted into each other, or created, as required, to fill the gaps, until the complete picture of a prototype modern economy began to emerge.

Initially the Revolution was a matter of marrying coal to iron; then, in its next stage, it concentrated on solving the problems of transporting the increasingly heavy machinery and the vast quantities of coal and ore required. In Shropshire, the configuration of the ground made water still, for a long time, the cheapest form of transport. In 1787 John Wilkinson, another Darby connection, ordered the construction of an iron barge, the *Trial*, which was made for him by a local master-smith, called 'John O'Lincoln'. It could carry thirty tons of ore or coal, and Wilkinson recorded: 'Yesterday week my iron boat was launched; it answers all my expectations, and has convinced all the unbelievers, who were 999 in 1,000. It will be a nine days' wonder, and will then be like Columbus's Egg.' In fact, the use of iron for water transport was as important for industry in the long run as the development of steam-railways, especially when steam-power could be installed in iron ships. The Shropshire rivers posed another kind of problem: how to cross them. By 1776, the Darby family realized that the extension of their collieries and iron-works on either side of the river made the replacement of the ferry by a bridge essential. They applied to Parliament for authority to build a bridge and took the dramatic step of casting it entirely in iron at their own works. Abraham Darby III supervised the design and casting himself, and reconstructed and enlarged one of his foundries to create it. Finished in 1779, with a span of one hundred feet, it was a brilliant achievement, the forerunner of modern large-scale engineering, and ocular evidence to visitors that Coalbrookdale was supreme in the new industrial world.

One visitor left an impression of Ironbridge, and the surrounding works, soon after the bridge was built: 'The flaming furnaces and smoking lime kilns form a spectacle horribly sublimb, while the stupendous iron arch, striding over the chasm, presents to the mind the idea of that fatal bridge, made by Sin and Death, over Chaos, from the boundaries of Hell to the wall of this now faceless world.' Here, then, were William Blake's 'Satanic mills', already vast and hideous, presaging an industrial world from which nature and beauty would – some thought – be irrevocably banished. On the other hand, there were those who found excitement and even poetry in the scene. Industrial England was built largely among hills – the hills which supplied the minerals and the water power which created it – and it was some decades before industrialism wholly scorched the untouched, primitive landscape from which it grew. Indeed, even today much of the industrial North and Midlands is still close to the wilderness. In a letter to her aunt, one of the Darby girls, Hannah, brought up near the forges, left a picture of her world, in the language of her Quaker faith:

Methinks how delightful it would be to walk with thee into fields and woods, then go into the Dale to view the works; the stupendous Bellows, whose alternate roars, like the foaming billows, is awful to hear; the mighty Cylinders, the wheels that carry on so many different branches of the works, is curious to observe; and many other things which I cannot enumerate; but if thou wilt come, I am sure thou would like it. It's really pleasant about our house, and so many comes and goes that we forget it's the Country till we look out at the window and see the woodland prospect.

The creation of a large-scale iron-casting industry in Shropshire was, of course, only one of many factors in the Industrial Revolution, though perhaps the key one. The 'miracle' had been brewing for 150 years; or, to use a metaphor from nuclear science, a number of conventional factors of economic growth had been drawing together, and in the late eighteenth century the resultant mass became 'critical' and the explosion took place, generating a chain-reaction which has followed ever since, and enveloped the world. Population, which had been a mere three million in the early sixteenth century, rose to over four million by 1600 and to an estimated five and a half million by 1650; by 1750 it had passed the six million mark, and thirty years later it was seven and a half million, and growing with accelerated speed as the death-rate continued to fall. The new masses supplied an ever-swelling army of recruits for the forges, mills and factories, the mines and workshops, driven from the land both by over-population and the higher wages they could earn in the industrial settlements. In turn, the towns which housed this rapid urban migration created new industries – the vast slate-mines of North Wales, the brick-works of the south Midlands. The revolution in agricultural techniques which began in the seventeenth century and continued steadily throughout the eighteenth, raised productivity on the land and enabled it to feed the additional millions even though the rural percentage of the population was falling fast – in 1830, when the first phase of the Industrial Revolution was over, ninety per cent of Britain's food was still home-grown. The establishment of efficient central banking in the last part of the seventeenth century, the growth of paper financial transactions and of the new sciences of insurance and statistics produced a steady decline in rates of interest and a rising volume in capital available for investment. General rates of interest dropped from ten per cent in late Stuart times to four per cent in 1727, and three per cent in 1757. Then, too, the growth of a world trading empire, opened up by the Royal Navy, established safe markets for British manufactures, especially cotton goods. More than any other product, cotton linked universal demand with new methods of mass production, made possible by the machinery which the iron-coal complexes turned out. Thus the 'take-off' phase of the

Industrial Revolution was marked by what we would now call an 'export-led boom'. In the first part of the eighteenth century, industries supplying mainly home demand increased output by seven per cent; export industries by seventy-six per cent. In the years 1750–70, the respective figures were seven and eighty per cent; after that point, the revolution took off, and export figures climbed astronomically; indeed, during the 1780s, all the economic indices took a sudden and sharply upwards turn.

At the Coalbrookdale works in 1785, during this period of rapid growth, there were sixteen 'Fire Engines', eight blast-furnaces, and twenty miles of railway. Iron was almost in the air, you could smell it everywhere; it was becoming a universal article. There are still, in the churchyard, many splendid cast-iron tomb-stones from these times, memorials to a primitive industrial age as well as to the ironmasters and their workpeople who lie beneath them. The church itself, built in 1796, was designed by Thomas Telford, the first architect-engineer (self-taught, like so many of the industrial pioneers) who had the imagination to grasp the aesthetic possibilities of the new techniques and who built roads, bridges, mansions, churches, chapels, ports and factories all over Britain.

Yet already there were hints of decadence. In 1762, Abraham Darby II signed the first price-fixing agreement with two other companies, in which they agreed to charge customers similar prices 'for all fire-engines, materials, cylinders and bored articles'. The new doctrines of absolute competition, and universal free trade, preached so avidly by Adam Smith, were meeting fixed and strenuous resistance. Economics itself bred its pessimists, who invented abstractions like the 'iron law of wages', and other tendentious obstacles to unrestricted economic growth. When, as inevitably happened, there were pauses in the growth of world trade, the manufacturers tended to panic and retrench, rather than invest in preparation for future expansions. Thus, during the post-Napoleonic recession, Joseph Reynolds, the son of Richard, simply closed down the Ketle works, and sold off the machinery; many others followed suit, there was mass-unemployment, and a third of the Shropshire banks failed. The rate of growth was not as spectacular as might have been expected, granted Britain's virtual monopoly of large-scale industry up till 1830. The Coalbrookdale Company raised its iron production from 24,900 tons in 1788 to 33,000 in the next decade; more than thirty years later it was still only 73,418 tons. Firms tended to remain self-financing, family affairs, content to settle for afflu-ence rather than open opportunities to mass-investment. Even as late as 1900 the overwhelming majority of British manufacturing concerns were private companies: investment capital tended to migrate abroad, even to build up rival centres of industry in the United States and Germany, rather than to reinforce the founda-tions of industrial supremacy which had been laid in Britain. Often the profits of industry were syphoned off into agricultural

The artist M. J. Newton has made these imaginative reconstructions from his observations of derelict machinery in the Coalbrookdale area. *Left* a headgear and *right* a horse gin.

estates, as successful manufacturers set themselves up as landed gentlemen; by the early nineteenth century their sons were turning their backs on the sources of the family wealth. So, for example, Richard Reynolds himself went into county society; and Sir Robert Peel, heir to the greatest of the cotton pioneers, became a squire, a Member of Parliament, a statesman and an art-collector, rarely setting foot inside a factory.

British industry bore the stigmata of its origins, when men created their works, by trial and error, from tiny workshops. Its units tended to remain small, highly-specialized, uncoordinated. Except in Coalbrookdale itself, throughout the Shropshire iron-coal fields, the forges which made wrought iron were not in the same locations as the furnaces which produced cast iron – they were, in fact, owned by different families as a rule. When, in the second quarter of the nineteenth century, Britain exported the capital, the patents, the techniques and the expert labour of the Industrial Revolution – to the United States, France, Germany and Belgium – these competitors were able to create industrial structures formed of much larger units, highly capitalized (often by state banks, as a matter of public policy), with the resources to devote a high percentage of turnover to

research and development. In these countries, not obsessed, like England, with the importance of class in education, a swelling army of science and engineering graduates emerged from the universities to form an industrial élite. So, by the 1870s, Britain had begun to lose the industrial leadership of the world, which it had acquired so overwhelmingly a century before.

By 1860 the Shropshire iron-industry was in relative decline. Total output had risen only from 111,000 tons to 145,000 since 1848, despite an unremitting expansion in world trade. By the 1880s, the British iron and steel industry was already overshadowed by its American and German rivals; and successful tycoons from Pittsburg, like Andrew Carnegie, were soon to appear to give condescending lectures on Britain's poor record of investment and its conservative unwillingness to replace ageing machinery. Then, too, in the Coalbrookdale area, the coal-seams were running out or becoming prohibitively expensive to work. This decline, for which both man and nature were responsible, ended the role of Shropshire as a forcing-house of industrial progress. But, as a compensation, it gives us today an unrivalled glimpse of industrial society in its primitive stage. The old works were not obliterated by newer models; they were simply aban-

Beauty or nightmare? The Industrial Revolution constituted a 'poignant and even poetic comment on man's insatiable appetite for wealth and power'.

doned, and allowed to fall into picturesque ruin. The winds of change moved elsewhere, leaving behind the archaeological detritus of the age of Newcomen, Watt and the Darbys, unvarnished and unadorned, except by the vegetation which has crept back, like the tropical jungle closing in on a doomed settlement. The place is a monument to the rise and decay of Industrial Man, a museum all the more vivid because it has not been tidied up and arranged by academic curators, but has assembled itself naturally under the irresistible forces of economic life. In its own way it is a national shrine, and one which holds an awesome warning for our future.

The Institution: 'something
of the setting and
atmosphere of a rich man's
house'.

11 THE ROYAL INSTITUTION

Science and 'the common purpose'

ALBEMARLE STREET, which runs into Mayfair from Piccadilly, is not an obvious site for a power-house of British science. In Queen Elizabeth's time Piccadilly itself was a high road leading out of London on the route to Bath and Bristol, though it was already a setting for the makers of fine ruffs and other luxury goods. In the seventeenth century, fashionable London spread northwards, and after the Restoration, Charles II's first Lord Chancellor, Edward Hyde, Earl of Clarendon, built a fine town house, overlooking the park which still bears his name. Around 1700 it was pulled down and replaced by Albemarle Street, described as consisting of 'excellent new Buildings inhabited by Persons of Quality'. Number 50, built in 1720 by Benjamin Jackson, who had worked as a mason for Wren and Vanbrugh, is one of London's finest early Georgian mansions, and for six generations it has housed the famous publishing firm of John Murray. Along the street, at Number 21, is the Royal Institution. It was refashioned, by Thomas Webster, when the British scientific community took it over in 1799. Later, in early Victorian times, it acquired a screen of giant Corinthian columns, to add to its dignity; and at the end of the century the house next door was acquired to provide more space. But the Lecture Theatre remains virtually as it was first conceived in 1800, and the Institution visibly retains something of the setting and atmosphere of a rich man's private house. It illustrates the tendency of the English to domesticate, to render cosy, even the most grandiose aspects of human progress.

This, indeed, is the way in which organized British science came into being. In 1645, a number of well-to-do and learned gentlemen formed the 'Philosophical or Invisible College': 'divers worthy persons', we are told, 'inquisitive into natural philosophy, and other parts of human learning, did, by agreement, meet weekly in London on a certain day, to treat and discourse of such affairs'. These weekly meetings grew into the Royal Society of London for Promoting Natural Knowledge – the RS, for short – patronized by royalty and great Whig magnates, including in its

Sir Joseph Banks, botanist, explorer, and co-founder of the Institution.

fellowship the leading figures in British seventeenth and eighteenth century science, promoting research and exploration, and propagating the scientific revolution inaugurated by the discoveries of its greatest member, Isaac Newton. But the RS was, almost by definition, an exclusive club of the learned, the rich and the well-born. It had little practical contact with the new industrial society to which Britain gave birth in the generation after 1770, a world shaped by little-educated ironmasters and cotton magnates, and by self-taught engineers and artisans – what Shakespeare had called 'the rude mechanicals'. There was no public provision for their education, no bridge between their practical, rule-of-thumb requirements, and the work of the theoretical scientists.

A remarkable polymath and man of affairs came forward to supply this bridge. Benjamin Thompson (1753–1814) was born in Massachusetts, and can thus be called an American; but during the Revolt of the Colonies he threw in his lot with George III, fought for him, and later advised the Colonial Office on American problems. He had been brought up as a shop-assistant, and though marriage to an heiress gave him leisure to follow his interests, he had no academic training. But he was eager to turn his hand to anything, seeing no true distinction between

176

knowledge as such, and the mechanical and organizational skill required to make it useful. He began by improving the quality of British gunpowder. Then he went to Bavaria, where he re-organized the army, established a modern armaments factory and a military academy, drew up a new poor law, introduced the potato, designed utilitarian kitchens and fireplaces, improved the breed of cattle and horses, and planted gardens. For a short time he was Prime Minister and Commander-in-Chief of the armed forces, and for his services was made a Count of the Holy Roman Empire, under the title of Count Rumford. For him, science was not an abstruse pursuit but the handmaiden of everyday life; he was an apostle of what, today, we would call 'intermediate technology'. In London, he made contact with Sir Joseph Banks (1744–1820), President of the Royal Society, another man of action who had used his wealth to finance Captain Cook's voyages, explore Africa, found the colony of New South Wales, and cultivate newly-discovered Pacific fruits for mass-consumption. In 1799 the two men set up the Royal Institution, 'for diffusing', as Rumford put it, 'the knowledge and facilitating the general introduction of useful mechanical inventions and improvements, and for teaching by courses of philosophical lectures and experiments the application of science to the common purposes of life'.

An admirable scheme: though perhaps fashionable Mayfair was not the best site for its headquarters. Indeed, the Institution has always had to struggle to fulfil its original purpose. Brilliant scientists are not easily fitted into any preordained pattern. As his first Professor of Chemistry, Rumford got a man after his own heart. Humphry Davy (1778–1829) was the son of a Cornish wood-carver, and learnt the rudiments of science as apprentice to a surgeon, and then as assistant to an eccentric physician, Dr Thomas Beddoes, who sought to cure his patients by getting them to inhale gases. Davy was a practical scientist who discovered the uses of 'laughing gas' (though surgeons were slow to employ it), designed the first safety lamp for miners, and helped to invent modern agriculture by his analyses of soils; his basic research in the chemistry of gases was equally distinguished. But, as a lecturer, he was too good, or rather too delightful. He was perhaps the handsomest man in the history of science, with a wonderful speaking voice, and his courses attracted not the rude mechanicals but the young ladies of Mayfair society. As one of them put it, 'those eyes were made for something besides poring over crucibles'; and when Davy was taken ill in 1807, the number of carriages bringing ladies to Albemarle Street (he lived at the Institute) to ask after him was so great that a slate was posted at the entrance giving hourly reports on his temperature. Davy became a notable figure in Regency London, married an heiress and won himself a baronetcy. He also, to do him justice, made the Institute the centre of world chemistry for more than a decade; but he did little to propagate science beyond London, WI.

Above Benjamin Thompson, Count Rumford, who, with Banks, established the Royal Institution and laid down the principles by which it was to be guided.

Above Humphrey Davy, the Royal Institution's first Professor of Chemistry who was 'perhaps the handsomest man in the history of Science'.

The Institute, indeed, faced a dilemma. It was not wealthy enough to give its lectures free. When they dealt with the more mundane applications of science, the number of subscribers dwindled, and the RI fell into debt. Davy, it is true, could attract the paying customer even to his discourses on tanning and agricultural chemistry; but no one else could. After 1812, he rarely lectured, and his successor, William Brande (1788–1866), though a distinguished chemist, had little public appeal. In the years after Waterloo, there was a real risk that the RI would have to close down for lack of funds. It was saved by the practical genius of Michael Faraday (1791–1867), perhaps the noblest and most likeable – as he was certainly the greatest – scientist the RI had fostered.

Faraday was a blacksmith's son from Surrey, who was apprenticed to a bookbinder. He seems to have acquired his passion for chemistry without professional assistance or encouragement of any kind, merely by reading books he picked up in his master's shop, and by attending free lectures. By chance, he was given a ticket to one of Davy's courses; and, by chance again, he got temporary employment as Davy's amanuensis when the great man injured his eyes in a chemical experiment. Fortunately, Davy's laboratory assistant got drunk and engaged in Brawling, and was dismissed. Faraday was invited to take his place, in the humble duties of 'fagging and scrubbing', and once inside the building he rapidly became indispensable. He had extraordinary facility with his hands, and devoted enormous care to the exact manipulative side of experiments, others' as well as his own; enormous pleasure, too – he bound his own books, some of which are in the RI Library. His career illustrates the principle that exact physical control, and sheer workmanship, are often as important in scientific advance as pure ratiocination. Faraday usually had to prepare his own materials, construct his apparatus, and operate and maintain his machinery. In his approach to science, there was no distinction between theoretical and applied work; nor, for that matter, any division in the branches of scientific knowledge. He hated such terms as 'chemist', 'physicist', and so forth, and called himself, to the end of his life, a Natural Philosopher. Indeed, his work was essentially in the borderland where physics, chemistry, and electrical and mechanical engineering merge. It was theoretical, in the sense that Faraday formulated the principles of modern experimentation, discovered the laws which governed the use of mechanically-created power in chemical analysis and synthesis, and created its terminology – electrolysis, ions, anode, cathode, and so forth. But he also built the first dynamo, and so opened up a world in which electricity became not just a wonder but a servant – the world of electric heating and lighting, of telegraphs and telephones, and ultimately of radio, TV and electronics.

Of course, it was the laboratory at the RI which made all this possible; and Faraday handsomely repaid this debt. He made the

Scientific Researches! — New Discoveries in PNEUMATICKS! — or — an Experimental Lecture on the Powers of Air 320

A Gillray cartoon (1802) illustrates 'an experimental lecture on the powers of Air'.

Institute the fulcrum of British scientific research, but he was always conscious that it had a larger purpose. After Davy's departure he kept the RI solvent by using the laboratory for industrial chemistry, carrying out work on steel alloys and thousands of analyses for commercial customers. But he rightly felt that this was not what the RI was for, and he deliberately set himself the task of becoming a professional lecturer, using the same principles of observation, analysis, experiment and preparation which he applied to his laboratory work. Unlike Davy, he had no natural gifts in this field; his early writings show he had difficulty in articulating on paper, let alone in front of an audience. He studied oratory: 'I am sorry to say that the generality of mankind cannot accompany us one short hour unless the path is strewn with flowers.' He paid careful attention to the seating arrangements in the lecture room, to the supply of fresh air, to the elimination of noisome smells (for a chemist, he had a curious hatred of smells, and often went around the RI sniffing and eliminating their source). The positioning of his illustrative experiments, the exact way in which they were carried out, their precise relationship to the purely verbal passages in his lectures were all a matter of intense study and constant modification. He spent five years preparing himself before he took the podium, and it is not surprising that he is one of the very few great lecturers

Aug 29th 1831.

1 Expts on the production of Electricity from Magnetism &c

2 Have had an iron ring made (soft iron), iron round and 7/8 inch
thick & ring 6 inches in external diameter — Wound many
coils of copper wire round one half, the coils being separated
by twine & calico — there were 3 lengths of wire each about 24
feet long and they could be connected as one length or used
as separate lengths. By trial with a trough each was
insulated from the other. Will call this side of the ring
A. On the other side but separated by an
interval was wound wire in two pieces
together amounting to about 60 feet in
length, the direction being as with the former
coils. this side call B.

3   Charged a battery of 10 pr plates 4 inches square. Made
the coil on B side one coil and connected its extremities by
a copper wire passing to a distance and just over a magnetic
needle (3 feet from iron ring) then connected the ends of one of
pieces on A side with battery: immediately a sensible effect on needle.
It oscillated & settled at last in original position. On breaking
connection of A side with Battery again a disturbance
of the needle

4   Made all the wires on A side one coil and sent
current from battery through the whole. Effect on needle much
stronger than before

5   The effect on the needle then but a very small force
that which the wire communicating directly with the battery

Left A page from Faraday's notebook – 'Experiments on the production of Electricity from Magnetism'.

who has succeeded in teaching others how to do it, for he certainly learnt the hard way himself. His notes to lecturers have the clarity and felicity of Shakespeare's advice to actors in *Hamlet*, for Faraday saw a lecture as an exercise in balance: a dramatic performance disciplined by the rules of aesthetic reticence, an exciting adventure, but one where truth was the hero and never the victim.

From 1825 until he retired in 1862, Faraday lectured constantly; his Friday Evening Discourses became a national institution. His subjects covered a prodigious range: theoretical chemistry in all its aspects, but also a great variety of practical matters, such as the artificial production of precious stones, magnetism, lighthouses, electric silk-looms, the ventilation of mines, the manufacture of mirrors and reflectors, zoology, botany, astronomy and geology. He lectured on contemporary marvels such as Brunel's tunnel under the Thames, and he was constantly reminding his audience that the function of research was to change human life for the better. 'To only think,' he said, 'of putting an electromagnetic machine into the *Great Western* or the *British Queen* and sending them across the Atlantic by it – or even the East Indies. What a glorious thing it would be!' He also gave special children's lectures in the school holidays, delighting his audiences by hurling a coal-scuttle in the air, where it was triumphantly drawn to the giant electro-magnet he had built.

Sometimes Faraday allowed himself while lecturing to speculate, to throw out ideas which he had not yet dared to put down on paper. For one of the Friday Discourses, he had invited Sir Charles Wheatstone to speak on the theory of sound. Sir Charles panicked just as the two of them were entering the Lecture Room, and ran out of the building. The omnicompetent Faraday, without notes, gave the gist of Sir Charles's lecture, and then went on, as he put it, to deliver his 'Thoughts on Ray Vibrations', the first hint of the electromagnetic theory of light. But, being a

Below One of Faraday's electro-magnets preserved at the Royal Institution.

Faraday lecturing: his range of subjects was vast, his energy prodigious, and 'his audience took fire with him, and every face was flushed'. This famous lecture took place on 27 December 1855 when the audience included the Prince Consort and his sons – the Prince of Wales and Prince Alfred.

practical man, he determined that the lecturer should not be allowed to decamp again; and, since then, the speaker has always been escorted from the library to the lecture-theatre, the Director of the Institution standing between him and the line of escape to the stairs.

Whether all those who flocked to Faraday's lectures appreciated the magnitude of his talents is hard to say. Foreign visitors particularly welcomed his self-taught clarity of speech: 'He articulates,' wrote a German professor, 'what other people swallow and chew.' There is no doubt that Faraday in full flow was a magnificent spectacle: he did not charm, like Davy, he – the metaphor is apt – electrified. 'It was an irresistible eloquence,' wrote Lady Holland, 'which waked the young from their visions and the old from their dreams . . . his enthusiasm sometimes carried him to the point of ecstacy . . . His hair streamed out from his head, his hands were full of nervous action, his light, lithe body seemed to quiver with its eager life. His audience took fire with him, and every face was flushed.' The tragedy is that, despite Faraday's creative powers, and his surpassing ability to teach, he was never given the opportunity to create a school of experimental chemistry. Britain had dominated chemical discovery from the days of Joseph Priestley (1733–1804) to Faraday's retirement. But it was in Germany, at the research institute founded by Faraday's contemporary, Justus Von Liebig, at Gliessen, that the practical harvest was garnered, and in the second half of the nineteenth century Germany and the United States took over from Britain the leadership of industrial chemistry and thus began the process whereby Britain has drifted down the economic league-tables of the world.

Indeed, Faraday's life, and his work at the RI, illuminates some of the more ominous aspects of Establishment attitudes to science in Britain. Even at the height of the Industrial Revolution, when the applications of science tripled Britain's wealth in a generation, and when British scientists were making incomparable contributions to human knowledge, they were very much outsiders in terms of the power-structure. Many of them came from Dissenting sects, and thus were excluded from the universities. Dr Beddoes, Davy's master, was driven from his post at Oxford because of his sympathies for the French revolution. Priestley, who had dared to print a reply to Burke's defence of the Bourbons, had his house and laboratory burnt down by a 'Church and King' mob, and barely escaped with his life; no one in the Establishment raised a finger to stop him emigrating to America, and he was honoured in every country except his own as one of the greatest men alive. Faraday himself was a member of an obscure sect, the Sandemanians, and thus excluded from academic honours. He had early learnt that the British class system, and British snobbery, were enemies of scientific progress. When he toured Europe as Davy's assistant, Sir Humphrey's rich wife tried to treat him as a servant-valet: 'She is haughty and proud to an excessive degree, and delights in making her inferiors feel her powers.' When, many years later, the Prime Minister, Lord Melbourne, summoned him to Downing Street and condescendingly offered him a pension (remarking that it was 'a piece of gross humbug'), Faraday left the room in disgust; it was not a question, he thought, of society honouring science with pensions, but of science honouring society by accepting them.

There was, indeed, a widespread feeling among professional scientists that, lacking official recognition, British science was falling behind. John Herschel, the astronomer, chemist and mineralogist, warned in 1830 that, in Britain, 'whole branches of Continental discovery are unstudied, and indeed almost unknown, even by name. It is vain to conceal the melancholy truth . . . in mathematics we have long since drawn the rein, and given over a hopeless race. In chemistry the case is not much better.' The same year, Charles Babbage published *Reflections on the Decline of Science in England* and set up an agitation for reform of the Royal Society, which he rightly castigated as a centre of social climbing, where titled amateurs were more highly regarded than creative professionals. The next year, a furious battle was fought over the presidency, the 'socialites' supporting the candidacy of Augustus, Duke of Sussex, fifth son of George III, a prince better known for his marital tangles than his familiarity with laboratories, while the 'professionals' voted for Herschel. The Duke won, by a vote of

Opposite Faraday seated on
the left of the picture with
other distinguished scientists.
From left to right Huxley,
Wheatstone, Sir David
Brewster, Professor Tyndale.

119:111, Faraday and most of those connected with the RI voting in the minority.

Faraday was not always in sympathy with Cassandras like Babbage who prophesied the imminent eclipse of British science. Distrusting over-specialization, he did not believe that the training of legions of industrial scientists necessarily brought better results in the long run: to divorce the practical applications of science from its theoretical exploration was, in his view, as pernicious as to pursue pure research without reference to the needs of the everyday world. But he certainly agreed with Babbage that the virtual absence of science-teaching in the universities and the leading schools was deplorable. It is, indeed, a reflection on the established educational system in eighteenth- and nineteenth-century England, almost entirely administered by Anglican clergymen, that it played no part in the formation of Britain's leading scientists. The physicist, Lord Rayleigh (1842–1919), stayed only one 'half' at Eton, and discovered his enthusiasm for science elsewhere (it was not, of course, taught at the college). Herschel was at Eton a few months, but came to science via the old-fashioned Euclid mathematics taught at Cambridge. Darwin was at Shrewsbury under the obscurantist Samuel Butler (grandfather of his more famous namesake) and recorded: 'Nothing could have been worse for the development of my mind than Doctor Butler's school.' All the rest went to non-public schools, chiefly the Dissenting Academies; or, like Faraday himself, since the primitive day-school he attended gave him nothing but 'the rudiments of reading, writing and arithmetic', were self-taught.

In some respects, and despite the efforts of the Royal Institution, the position grew worse in the mid-century, for the admission of non-Anglicans to the university led many parents to transfer their children from Dissenting Academies to the public schools which alone taught the dead-language syllabus necessary to gain admission to Oxbridge. Thus Brunel, for example, a brilliant product of the Nonconformist educational system, sent his sons to Harrow, which excluded from its curriculum virtually all knowledge which had not already been available to a well-educated citizen of imperial Rome. Faraday, engaged at the Institution in propagating scientific knowledge, yet excluded from any influence on the educational system as such, watched in important amazement the unavailing efforts of the reformers to find a place for science in the august, and heavily endowed, seats of English learning. In the early 1860s, a Royal Commission was at last appointed to inquire into the curricula of the Public Schools, but it was forced to listen to a passionate defence of Greek and Latin studies by the leading votaries of the teaching profession. Dr George Moberley, the Headmaster of Winchester, hotly opposed the introduction of science: 'A boy who has learned grammar,' he told the Commissioners, 'has learned to talk and to write in all his life; he has possessed himself for ever of an

instrument of power. A man who has learned the laws of electricity has got the facts of science, and when they are gone, they are gone for ever.'

Such arguments mystified Faraday. How could the 'facts of science' be said to 'go'? Anyway, there was no such thing as 'the facts of science'. There were no 'facts' to be crammed into a child, in the same way as Greek and Latin words. No scientist could believe in the finite nature of knowledge. On the contrary, scientific awareness was a consciousness of the possibility of error: man existed, would always exist, in a confusing and ever-changing admixture of truth and falsehood: the whole purpose of scientific training and method was to enable him to distinguish between truth and error. The virtue of scientific education was that it inculcated a disciplined habit of criticism and self-criticism, and turned the mind not into a repository of received knowledge and opinions, but into a creative force. As he put it to the Commissioners:

... if the term education may be understood in so large a sense as to include all that belongs to the improvement of the mind either by the acquisition of the knowledge of others or by increase of it through its own exertions, we learn by them what is the kind of education science offers to man. It teaches us to be *neglectful* of nothing – not to despise the small beginnings, for they precede of necessity all great things in the knowledge of science, either pure or applied. It teaches a continual comparison of the *small* and the *great*, and that under differences almost approaching the infinite: for the small as often contains the great in principle as the great does the small; and thus the mind becomes comprehensive. It teaches to deduce principles carefully, to hold them firmly, or to suspend the judgment – to discover and obey *law* and by it to be bold in applying to the greatest what we know of the smallest ... The beauty of electricity, or of any other force, is not that the power is mysterious or unexpected ... but that it is under *law*, and that the taught intellect can even now govern it largely. The human mind is placed above, not beneath it; and it is in such a point of view that the mental education afforded by science is rendered supereminent in dignity, in practical application, and utility; for, by enabling the mind to apply the natural power through law, it conveys the gifts of God to man.

Faraday took the issue with great seriousness because he realized that the Royal Institution could not, by itself, transform the scientific education of the country: that could only be done by public authority, working through the regular system of schools and colleges. His eloquence unhappily did not persuade the Royal Commissioners; their recommendations for the introduction of science teaching were unambitious, and were rendered nugatory by the hostility of headmasters. Not until Dr F. W. Sanderson went as headmaster to Oundle at the close of the nineteenth century did the public schools begin to take science seriously. Worse, in the meantime, the new state schools which sprang up in the wake of the 1870 Education Act tended to imitate, on a humbler scale, the syllabuses and teaching attitudes of the old foundations, for the state inspectors who, in effect, controlled them, were themselves imbued with the public school classical tradition.

Nevertheless, within the limits of its powers, the Royal Institution struggled hard to bring into existence a scientifically-aware public, and, not least, to widen the channels of communication between scientists themselves, and the proliferating varieties of technicians, engineers and 'mechanicals' who were creating the modern world. It was as a result of Faraday's work at the RI, and the abortive attempt to reform the Royal Society, that the British Association for the Advancement of Science came into existence: a body run by professionals for professionals, which eliminated the political manoeuvring and social-climbing of the Royal Society. Its great annual meetings made possible the wide diffusion of a mass of scientific papers, drew the attention of government to the needs of British science, and acted as its platform to the world. The regular work of the Institute continued, under such men as John Tyndall, Sir Edward Frankland and Lord Rayleigh. What impresses us today is the range of their activities – almost as wide as Rumford's own – and the way in which they kept in view their founders' concept of the close relationship between science and everyday life. Frankland was not merely a chemist and astronomer, but a practical expert on sanitation. Rayleigh was a mathematician, a physicist, a sound-engineer and a superb organizer of scientific work – as well as a highly-successful agriculturalist and estate-manager. Tyndall was a chemist, a physicist, a botanist, a meteorologist and a geologist, a scientific adviser to the Board of Trade, a Trinity House consultant, a pioneer in glacierology – and, not least, one of the first of the mountaineer-scientists.

There is, indeed, something in the atmosphere of the Royal Institution – perhaps the fact that it is housed in the middle of a great metropolis, and in constant contact with the public, rather than isolated in a university campus – which allows it to embody the salient principle that science is part of life. Its existence, and its history, may help to explain the fact that Britain, despite its relative decline as an industrial power, still ranks second only to the United States as a pioneering scientific nation.

12 BRIGHTON
The Pursuit of Pleasure

THROUGHOUT recorded history men and women have gone to hot springs for their health, but it has taken them a lot longer to recognize the merits (and delights) of sea bathing. It seems to have been a seventeenth-century discovery, with Scarborough as its first beneficiary. Brighton's emergence as a resort, a generation later, came about very largely by accident. It had been, since early Saxon times, a fairly prosperous fishing town, built on low cliffs at the point where the Wellsbourne emerged from the downs, and flowed over a stony valley, called the Steine, into the Channel. In November 1703, what was probably the worst storm in English history destroyed the cliffs, and another storm two years later completed the damage. All the lower town was swept away, and to save what was left of Brighton, groynes were hastily built to collect protective barriers of shingle. The unforeseen consequence was that Brighton acquired a bathing beach.

By the 1730s, the first visitors were coming to take the 'bathing cure', most of them recommended by Dr Richard Russell, a leading physician in the county town, Lewes. In these early years Brighton was cheap. The Revd William Clarke, Rector of Buxted, who came in 1736, tells us he rented two bedchambers, two sitting-rooms and a pantry for 5s a week. In winter, the town was only accessible by sea, and even in summer it was regarded as a very cut-off place. Things began to change when Dr Russell decided to give up general practice and operate his own sanatorium in Brighton. In 1753 he built Russell House, just above the beach, on the site of what is now the Royal Albion Hotel. Russell was not a quack. Like most of the best British doctors in the early eighteenth century, he had studied medicine at Leyden, and his researches had won him a Fellowship of the Royal Society before he moved to Brighton. He believed sea-water could cure asthma, cancer, deafness, tuberculosis and rheumatism, and he had written a textbook, mainly pirated from Dutch sources, known as *Russell on Sea-Water*. His patients bathed daily, but they also drank the water. A pint of Brighton sea-water, noted Russell, 'would be commonly sufficient in a grown person to

A bathing machine designed by the Quaker Benjamin Beale which, with its discreet modesty-hood, dealt with 'inquisitive males who studied the beaches through telescopes'.

give three or four sharp stools'. They took the water with Russell's patent mixture of coral, crab's eyes, burnt sponge, snakeflesh, seafood and 'prepared wood lice'. Russell also insisted on relaxing exercises, plenty of fresh air, and loose, light-weight clothes. Hence, if his treatment could not live up to all his claims, most of his patients stood to benefit. The iodine they absorbed from the air and the water helped to cure goitre and related complaints, which were very common in those days. They became, perhaps for the first time in their lives, really clean: and many diseases were caused, or aggravated, by dirt. Almost incidently, they discovered that sea-bathing was delightful.

The first bathing machine made its appearance at Brighton in 1735. The local fishermen (they were called 'bathers') hauled the machine down the beach and their wives, called 'dippers', ducked the patients in the sea. Machines were used chiefly by ladies, as they acted as a mobile changing-room and afforded some protection from vulgar onlookers. Indeed, in the 1770s, a Margate Quaker, Benjamin Beale, invented a modesty-hood for the machines, to deal with the threat of inquisitive males who studied the beaches through telescopes. It is clear that, in the eighteenth century at least, most women bathed naked, as they had been doing at spas like Bath and Buxton for centuries. The men were invariably naked, whether or not they bathed from machines. But evidently at Brighton the custom was gradually established that certain parts of the beach were subject to rules: thus, in 1807, the parish meeting protested against 'the indecent practice of indiscriminate bathing in front of the town', and two years later a local tradesman was fined for 'having daily exposed himself naked on the beach'. Unless a machine was used, naked bathers of both sexes were encouraged to swim out of eyeshot of the town – as at St Tropez today. But male bathing-costumes were not adopted until the 1860s, when they arrived from France and were called '*caleçons*'. Even so, a good deal of naked bathing went on in Victoria's heyday, though the custom evidently varied from one resort to another, as we learn from the diary of the Revd Francis Kilvert. At Weston-Super-Mare, 5 September 1872, he notes: 'There was a delicious feeling of freedom in stripping in the open air and running down naked to the sea . . . the red morning sunshine glowing upon the naked limbs of the bathers.' At Shanklin, the next year, he found himself forced 'to adopt the detestable custom of bathing in drawers. If ladies don't like to see men naked why don't they keep away from the sight?' However, in 1874, just out of sight of Shanklin, he found nudity still in full swing: 'One beautiful girl stood entirely naked on the sand . . . there was the supple, slender waist, the gentle dawn and tender swell of the bosom and budding breasts . . . above all the soft and exquisite curves of the rosy dimpled bottom and broad white thigh.'

There can be no doubt that the sexual element played an enormous part in Brighton's success. Indeed, the doctors who recommended sea-bathing did not scruple to hint that it was a sure specific for flagging sexual desire. Thus, as one of Russell's flackmen put it (neatly inverting the cold-bath theory of Victorian public schools), 'Cold bathing has this good alone: it makes old John to hug old Joan'. Dr John Awsiter, who succeeded Russell as Brighton's leading physician, specialized in the elderly, for whom he built an indoor bath-house in 1769 to save them the rough and tumble of the beach; and he openly claimed that sea-water cured impotence. He also served women patients with a mixture of sea-water, milk and cream of tartar – a briny yoghurt – which, among other things, dealt with barrenness. Another leading Brighton doctor, the Irishman Anthony Relhan, claimed that the very air and sunshine of Brighton stimulated the sexual appetite.

At all events, it was undoubtedly sex which attracted the future Prince Regent to Brighton. Royalty had been there before: the Duke of Gloucester in 1765 and the Prince's uncle, the Duke of Cumberland, in 1771. But in the 1760s Brighton was still a comparatively primitive place. Lodgings were described as 'execrable', and though, from 1766, there were twice-weekly balls at the George Inn, and two circulating libraries where ladies and gentlemen came to gossip in the daytime, there was a lack of polite society. Dr Johnson, who came twice in the mid-1760s, found it monstrously dull: 'Your wits get blunted for want of some other mind to sharpen them upon.' Judging Brighton, as he did most places, by the quantity of timber in the area, he pronounced against: 'The town is so truly desolate that if one had a mind to hang oneself for desperation at being obliged to live in it, it would be difficult to find a tree on which to fasten the rope.'

But a marked change seems to have come in 1771, when not only Cumberland, but the Duke of Marlborough came for the summer. The latter bought a property on the west side of the Steine, which was now grassed over and used as a promenade

Health and high society. People flocked to Brighton to take the waters and to see 'who walks with who'. The Aquarium in the 1880s.

for the gentry, and he entertained lavishly, keeping a staff of forty. This season launched Brighton as a resort for celebrities. Wilkes came there four times. Gibbon found 'the air gives health, spirits and a ravenous appetite'. Fanny Burney came to stay with the Thrales, 'who live on the Steine, where they indulge the pleasure of viewing, all day long, who walks with who'. In 1775, Brighton's oldest inn, the Old Ship, built a second set of Assembly Rooms, to rival the George, and both establishments were placed under the command of a newly-appointed Master of Ceremonies, Captain Wade, who had been trained in his duties at Bath. Balls were held on Mondays at the George and on Thursdays at the Ship; cards were played on the other four week-nights, and on Sundays there was a promenade and 'public tea'. Visitors obtained access to this social round by putting down their names in the visitor's books, kept at the circulating libraries, as soon as they arrived. The MC then called on them at their lodgings and, when satisfied of their gentility, extracted a subscription of a guinea (this entitled them to the cheap-rate entry to the balls at 3s 6d, tea or coffee included, instead of the standard 5s), issued them with invitation cards and arranged introductions. Apart from the Assembly Rooms, life revolved round the libraries, which were in effect public clubs, where discreet gambling took place; and gambling was a feature of many Brighton shops, where ladies rattled dice for smuggled lace and other French dainties. Visitors could also gamble on the bullbaiting which went on at West Brighton (now Hove) until 1810, or cockfighting, which flourished in Brighton itself until the following year. And, from 1783, the Duke of Richmond, one of the local magnates, sponsored horseracing.

The occasion of the Prince Regent's first visit was this inaugural Brighton race-meeting, and to attend it he stayed with his Uncle Cumberland on the Steine. But, says his contemporary biographer Robert Huish, he lingered on in Brighton not for health reasons but because of 'the angelic figure of a sea-nymph whom he one day encountered reclining on one of the groynes on the beach'. This was Charlotte Fortescue, described as 'pretty', but 'illiterate and ignorant'. The Prince was just twenty-one, and already well launched on a disastrous career of philandering.

The affair with Miss Fortescue did not endure; but, during it, Brighton captured the Prince's imagination. For the next season he determined to have a property of his own, and in the spring of 1784 sent down his Clerk of the Kitchens, Louis Weltje, on a purchasing mission. The Prince's employment of this former gingerbread maker and street peddlar to handle his property deals was very characteristic. However, the German was a shrewd operator; he acquired on his own account several fine houses in London and Brighton, and when he finally left the Prince's service entertained in great style, boasting to his guests: 'Dish ish moine, dat ish moine; and, what ish more, I can leave it all to my

Below The Prince Regent discovers Brighton – Rex Whistler's interpretation of his meeting with 'the angelic figure of a sea-nymph whom he one day encountered reclining on one of the groynes on the beach'.

Overleaf Brighton: *The Old Chain Pier* by Turner (*1775–1851*).

posteriors.' For the Prince's use, Weltje acquired a house on the fashionable west side of the Steine.

This house gradually expanded, through further acquisitions, into a property of eight acres, and over a period of thirty-five years was transformed into the Royal Pavilion. The Prince's building and decorating activities were almost continuous, because even when no major scheme was in hand he was constantly changing the interiors. The creation of the Pavilion covered the years of his clandestine marriage with the Catholic Mrs Fitzherbert in 1785, his separation from her and his official marriage to Caroline of Brunswick in 1794; his break with

The Royal Pavilion.

Caroline and the reign of Lady Jersey in 1796; his reunion with Mrs Fitzherbert in 1800; his final separation from her in 1811, and the reigns of his last mistresses, Lady Hertford and Lady Conyngham. All these ladies lived, at various times, either in the emerging Pavilion or, for the sake of decency, in rented houses nearby, reputedly connected to the Prince's quarters by tunnels. Life in the Pavilion cannot have been entirely agreeable, because it was in a constant state of flux. In 1787, the Prince had the original house pulled down and replaced by a small palladian villa, designed by Henry Holland, which launched the sea-side style of curved bay windows and iron balconies. To mark his

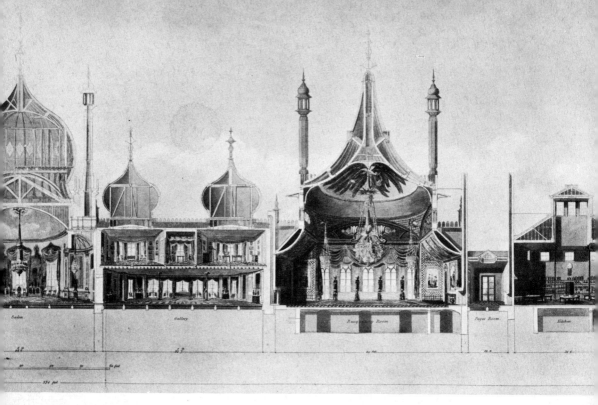

A cross-section of the Pavilion by Nash; the original building was expanded, reconstructed and made increasingly elaborate over a period of thirty-five years.

reconciliation with Mrs Fitzherbert, the Prince had the villa pulled down and replaced by what was termed a 'cottage orné', designed by P. F. Robinson, an expert in the picturesque style, who had already built the 'Swiss Cottage' in St John's Wood and the Egyptian Hall in Piccadilly. Before the rustic cottage was finished, the Prince had been captivated by the Oriental vogue started by the publication, in 1800, of Thomas Daniell's six-volume *Views of Oriental Scenery*. The interiors were thus painted, papered and furnished in the Chinese style, and in 1803 the Prince built a stable block and riding house (now the Dome) in the shape of a Moslem-Indian mosque. From 1806 he was planning to tear down the main building and re-erect it in the Indian fashion, a scheme finally carried through by John Nash in the years 1816–22. Few of the Prince's contemporaries were impressed by the results. Princess Lieven called it 'the Kremlin', what she termed 'a mixture of Moorish, Tartar, Gothic and Chinese, all in stone and iron; it is a whim which has already cost £700,000 and is still not fit to live in.' Others thought it 'a nondescript monster' or a 'madhouse'; and John Wilson Croker, the Tory MP, dismissed it as 'an absurd waste of money, which will be a ruin in half a century or sooner'.

Yet the interiors, over which the Prince took enormous trouble, sometimes altering the decorative schemes five or six times before he was satisfied, were undoubtedly impressive. Even Croker found the kitchen 'admirable – such contrivances for roasting, boiling, baking, stewing, frying, steaming and heating; hot plates, hot closets, hot air and hot hearths, with all manner of cocks for hot and cold water, and warm water and steam, and twenty

198

saucepans all ticketed and labelled, placed up to their necks in a vapour bath'. The dining-room occupied what had once been the space of the whole original villa, and there was a grand drawing-room for balls, plus two others for cards – and, above all, a circular music-room, where the seventy-piece royal band played. There, in 1823, Rossini conducted his *Thieving Magpie* overture and selections from *The Barber of Seville*.

In his younger days, the Prince used the villa for drinking-orgies, especially when the Tenth Duke of Norfolk, known as 'Jockey', came over from Arundel Castle as his guest. But Thomas Creevey, who had taken part in them, noted a distinct quietening down of the royal life style after Mrs Fitzherbert came back in 1800: both she and her husband were now tightly-laced, 'and their affection seems to grow with their growth and fatten with their fat'. Dinner was at six; afterwards, there was music and card-playing; sandwiches were handed round at eleven-thirty, and the Pavilion was cleared by midnight.

Below The Pavilion kitchen 'such contrivances for roasting, boiling, baking, stewing, frying, steaming and heating'.

As a young man the Prince had bathed in the sea from time to time – there is a print of him entering a machine in full army uniform – and patronized the steam-baths which Sheikh Deen Mahomed, the 'Brighton Shampooing Surgeon' had opened on

the Front. 'Shampooing' was the contemporary word for massage, and Mahomed not only conducted his parlour with success (it was run by his descendants until 1870) but superintended the Prince's bath-room at the Pavilion. As the Prince aged, however, his activities narrowed. 'I have known HRH here six or seven years,' wrote Croker in 1818, 'and never saw or heard his being on foot outside the limits of the Pavilion, and in general he avoids even riding through the principal streets.' Even at the age of thirty-three he weighed seventeen stone, and by the time he became Regent in 1811 he had to use what was called a 'Merlin Chair' to get about. His private rooms were transferred to the ground floor to avoid the use of stairs, he was lifted on to his horse by ropes and pulleys, and an inclined plane was necessary to get him into one of Mahomed's baths. By the mid-1820s, now King, he found the Pavilion an increasing embarrassment: it had no grounds, properly speaking, and its low windows made his movements observable from the street: all Brighton, said Croker, could watch the King pay his daily visits to Lady Conyngham's quarters. He was so fat that he would summon his valet 'forty times during the night' to tell him the time from the watch which hung by his bed, and from 1828 he was ashamed to show himself in Brighton any more. Two years later he died at Windsor.

An early nineteenth-century print of the parlour run by Sheikh Deen Mahomed. He specialized in massages, at that time called 'shampooing'.

His younger brother, William IV, used the Pavilion every summer, though the dinners became spartan and the invitations rarer. But Victoria did not find it to her taste. It lacked the privacy she craved. In October 1838 her diary records a conversation with Lord Melbourne: 'Spoke of my dislike to go to Brighton; and he said "I wouldn't go there if I didn't like it". Said, as I had a Palace there I thought it was necessary I should go; he said, not at all, for that it was only a fancy of George IV's to go there, nobody ever went there before. Said I thought it would vex the people if I didn't.' The advent of Albert, and their joint discovery of the Highlands, settled the matter: in 1849 Victoria sold the Pavilion to the Brighton corporation, and to the consternation of the citizens insisted on removing all the interior fittings, leaving the place gutted and desolate.

But in the meantime Brighton had become a great international resort and, next to Bath, architecturally the most distinguished city in the kingdom. The first major set-piece, the Royal Crescent, went up in 1798, and it remains Brighton's greatest charm, for its elegant lines have a true nautical flavour, faced with gleaming black tiles to resist wind-driven rain and spray. The main building period began in the 1820s, when Kemp Town and Brunswick Town carried the city to east and west, and inaugurated a new style in town-planning. The inspiration came from the terraces Nash was putting up around Regent's Park, but the architects – Charles Busby, Aaron Wilds, and his son Aaron Henry Wilds, were local – and the broad bay windows, with their vast expanse of glass and elaborate railings and blinds, were *sui generis*. In early Victorian times, the Brighton skyline, seen from the end of the chain-pier which was opened in 1823, was unique in the world: a configuration of crescents, terraces, squares and avenues, not golden-brown as in Bath, but painted brilliant white and cream, which made up an idealized maritime city of pleasure.

The skyline, moreover, was enlivened increasingly by the spires and towers of scores of churches; for, if society came to Brighton to bathe, it remained to pray – after a fashion. The rise of Brighton coincided with the dawn of religious toleration, and the eruption of new styles of worship, within and without the established church. But there was no nonsense about egalitarianism when religion came back into social favour. The first of the new churches was built in 1793 'for the use of such of the inhabitants as are disposed to become purchasers of pews'. Indeed, some of these 'proprietory chapels', as they were called, were pure financial speculations. A portion of the pew-rents was allocated as a stipend for the curate, the rest went straight to the owner-proprietor. The freeholds could be bought and sold. Occasionally free pews were provided for the poor in the gallery; or the poor were segregated in the nave, and the galleries divided into expensive boxes. Some churches banned non-paying worshippers altogether. An example of the proprietory church was St Margaret's, built by Bernard Gregory, owner of the *Brighton*

Gazette and the scurrilous London *Satirist*, who had served a year in gaol for criminal libel.

In the mid-Victorian period, the proprietors were bought out, and a more altruistic religious revival, with distinct High Church tendencies, got under way. St Paul's Church, in West Street, built by R. C. Carpenter, the architect of Lancing, was notorious for its ritual and incense, and a low-church pamphlet denounced its services as 'the Sunday opera in St Paul's'. St Michael's was built as a double church, with splendid interior fittings and decorations by Morris, Burne-Jones, Rossetti and Romaine Walker. It was followed by St Martin's, designed by Somers Clark in 1875, and, biggest of all, by St Bartholomew's in Anne Street, designed by Edmund Scott, with a nave four feet higher than Westminster Abbey. Like most of Brighton's remarkable buildings, its appearance aroused violent controversy, being variously described as 'a cheese warehouse', 'a brick parallelogram' and 'a Noah's ark in brick'.

Virtually all these churches, ranging from late-Georgian to high Victorian Gothic, and incorporating architectural fancies culled from all over Europe and the East, have found passionate modern defenders. But their return to fashion came too late in many cases. In the first half of the twentieth century, the receding tides of religious belief left them stranded and empty. St Margaret's, for instance, was demolished in 1959; the 'High and Dry' Church of the Resurrection became a meat store, then a depository for beer barrels; and the fine North Street Methodist chapel, built by the famous Countess of Huntingdon in 1791, was pulled down as recently as 1968. There were other lamentable victims. Some chapels progressed down the social scale, and became centres for revivalist cults, which flourished mightily among lower-middle class Brighton ladies. At the Adullam Chapel, the Revd Henry Prince advocated 'spiritual marriages' with 'soul mates', and acquired a fortune of £30,000 and a harem of pious women, whom he took to his 'Abode of Love' in Somerset. Another religious eccentric, John William Wood, staged ritual dances, culminating in bouts of hysteria, in his 'Ark of the Living God'; he was eventually stoned out of Brighton by an outraged mob, and left shouting: 'To Hell with ye who persecute me. Devils await ye, generations of vipers!' If some of Brighton's nineteenth-century churches have gone, many remain and even flourish: Brighton still offers a wider spread of Christian places of worship, and a bigger variety of sub-Christian cults, than any other place in the kingdom, except London itself.

Brighton had grown up as essentially a resort for the rich, and those who wished to ape them. For Londoners of modest means it was much less accessible than Margate or Southend. It is true that the vigorous could ride there and back in a day: the Prince Regent, as a young man, did so on at least one occasion, taking nine hours. The Royal Mail coaches, started in 1784, had cut the regular London–Brighton run to eight hours by 1810, and soon

Brighton Belles as seen by Cruikshank (1826). By this time Brighton was well established as the most fashionable resort in England.

up to fifty coaches a day travelled the route. Crack coaches, like
the 'Brighton Age' and the 'Red Rover', often driven by 'sporting
baronets', got the time down to four-and-a-half hours. But this
mode of travel was very expensive: the poor went by wagon,
taking two days.

The big change, which transformed Brighton life, was the
coming of the London railway in 1841. It was a major piece of
engineering, taking three years to build at a cost of £3 million,
and involving a series of cuttings, tunnels and viaducts. They
bore the marks of the riotous taste beloved of Victorian railway
engineers, embellished with Gothic turrets, Egyptian arches and
Roman columns, and culminating in the dramatic viaduct which
bring the line into Brighton station, itself carved out of the side
of the Dyke Road ridge: a concept consciously planned to
imitate a Roman aqueduct painted by Claude. The trains
themselves were luxuriously conceived: the expresses, confined to

Right The Grand Hotel has now changed. In more elegant days this was only one of the many great houses which were built to accommodate Brighton's prosperous clientele.

Below Brighton beach. The skyline has changed, the popularity remains. 'Brighton is a battered beauty, but a beauty none the less.'

first-class fares, and taking a mere one-and-three-quarter hours, were run in the hope that 'the railways would be transporting the most respectable and the highest families in the Kingdom to the resort'. In fact, they soon proved the means whereby the London working man could enjoy Brighton: day-trips and cheap excursions brought the poor in multitudes. Soon after the turn of the century, the motor-coach, which made its appearance in Brighton as early as 1905, confirmed the trend.

Fast modern transport is a great mingler and leveller of classes. From being an exclusive resort, Brighton soon became what it is today, a place where anyone can find entertainment to suit his taste and his pocket. With the withdrawal of royal patronage (briefly and unsuccessfully restored under Edward VII), High Society went elsewhere, to the Highlands and the Continent. But Brighton continued to attract celebrities, especially in the arts. Byron had come there as long ago as 1807, accompanied by his boxing tutor, the All-England champion 'Gentleman Jack', and a cockney beauty dressed in boy's clothes, who referred to her patron as 'my bruvver'. To Brighton came Thackeray to write *Vanity Fair*, and Dickens to write *Dombey and Son* and *Bleak House*. Arnold Bennett used the Royal York Hotel as his headquarters while conceiving *Clayhanger* and *Hilda Lessways*, and Brighton was also patronized by Harrison Ainsworth, Henry James and D. H. Lawrence, in addition to dispossessed foreign notables like Metternich, King Louis Philippe and Napoleon III. Vast public palaces went up to accommodate such swells: the Royal York (1819), the Bedford (1820), the Royal Albion (1826), the Grand (1864), and the Metropolitan (1890). But it was, above all, the theatrical profession which filled the gap left by royalty. Theatre had flourished in Brighton since the 1770s, and the opening of the Theatre Royal in 1807, with Charles Kemble as *Hamlet*, marked its emergence as a leading centre of provincial drama. The town quickly became, and remains, the most reliable testing-ground for West End productions, and actors came there increasingly not just to perform but to relax and to live. With them, of course, came the less reputable elements of the entertainment industries. As early as 1810 it had been noted that, by October, 'The Paphian Temples at Brighton are now quite deserted, the presiding goddesses having taken their flight to dispense their favours in the more polluted brothels of the Metropolis'. Successful chorus-girls, rich bookies, the racing-gangs of Graham Greene's *Brighton Rock*, became familiar figures on the scene, as well as the wealthy seeking a quick divorce: 'Mr and Mrs Smith' appeared.

With its constantly changing role in the national life, it was, perhaps, impossible to preserve Brighton as a perfect artifact of early nineteenth-century architecture and taste. The wonder is, rather, that so much of it remains. In 1935, a concrete twelve-storey block of flats drove the first wedge into the Georgian sea-front panorama. Sir Herbert Carden, knighted for his services as mayor, and called 'The Father of Modern Brighton', wanted to replace all the crescents and squares by modern flats and hotels, and dismissed the Pavilion itself as 'a complete anachronism in the modern age'. Bombing and accident did their work, a notable loss being the destruction of the classical Bedford Hotel by fire in 1964; and throughout the 1950s and 1960s property developers were removing Regency and Georgian buildings, though against a rising volume of protest. Virtually all the post-war creations in Brighton are undistinguished, and many are hideous. Part of the skyline remains, but its continuity and scale has been mutilated by multi-storey slabs. On the other hand, the Pavilion has been restored in all its glory, and there are still in Brighton scores of streets, pubs, churches and shops which conjure up an age when the pursuit of pleasure went hand-in-hand with elegance, and when raffishness contrived to exclude vulgarity. Brighton is a battered beauty, but a beauty nonetheless; and we can still see what Thackeray meant when he described it as 'a clean Naples, with genteel *lazzaroni*'.

Overleaf left Pegwell Bay by William Dyce (*1806–64*), a forerunner of the Pre-Raphaelites.

Overleaf right Dover Castle: for centuries the Watchdog of the Channel.

13 THE ENGLISH CHANNEL

'Masters of the Narrow Sea'

IT IS ARGUABLE that the English Channel is the most important single geographical fact in history, since it made possible the process of separate development in England which produced both the Industrial Revolution and parliamentary democracy. Yet in geological terms, the Channel is a very recent creation. In Palaeolithic times, Britain was linked to the Continental land-mass. South-east England was an extension of the huge north European plain, with what is now the Channel forming merely one of a series of gentle valleys; a chalk ridge linked Kent and Picardy; and the Thames was, very likely, a tributary of the Rhine. The southern part of the Channel already existed, as a huge inlet, the coast following what is now the thirty-fathom contour, being steadily eaten into by the sea. Sometime in the Mesolithic or Neolithic Ages, about eight thousand years ago, by a process of erosion and subsidence, a breach was finally created:

The white cliffs of Dover; the Channel separating Britain from the European mainland is, arguably, 'the most important single geographical fact in history'.

the Anglo-German plain was flooded, and became the southern North Sea, with the Thames acquiring its proper status as a sea-river, and the last link in the Kent–Picardy ridge collapsed. As there was, and is, a big difference in the time of the high tide coming round Scotland into the North Sea, and the high water coming up the Channel direct from the Atlantic, the breach must have been widened with dramatic speed – one of the great 'happenings' of pre-history – with the Channel becoming impassable, except by boat, within the memory of a single family.

The speed at which the Channel enlarged itself soon slowed down, to a few feet per century in historic times. But it still continues, inexorable, as the sea batters at the soft chalk cliffs. Indeed, the Channel is changing all the time, and so modifying the lives of those who live on its littoral. While the cliffs are being eroded, deposits of shingle are forming, and creating promontories: two thousand years ago the site of the vast nuclear power-station at Dungeness was covered in thirty or forty feet of seawater. In the southern part of the Channel, where the rocks are much older and harder, the coastline has scarcely changed at all; but from the Isle of Wight to Kent, it has been transformed. There have been major recoveries of land, between Hythe and Hastings, in Pevensey Bay, and between Thanet and the Kent Coast. On the other hand, former islands have been reduced to rocks, or submerged completely. Subsidence created the Isle of Wight, and erosion is still diminishing it: the Needles were once much more formidable rocks, as early prints and drawings show. The main sea-route from Dover and the Channel to London once ran through the Wantsum Channel, between the Kent Coast and the Isle of Thanet, which is now dry land. Even as little as a thousand years ago, the coasts of Kent, Sussex and Hampshire were extremely ragged, with scores of islands and hundreds of inlets: since then, human efforts to prevent nature from redrawing the map have smoothed the outline.

In the past it has been assumed that pre-Roman Britain was subjected to periodic Continental waves of settlement, identified by the burial goods of the people and dated by relating these articles to Continental archetypes. Thus bronze was brought across the Channel about 2,000 BC, iron about 500 BC, and so forth; the process culminating with the arrival of the Belgae in the century before Caesar's landing. But new methods of carbon-dating are undermining the diffusionist view that all cultures spread from a single point of origin; and it may be that these prehistoric 'invasions' are imaginary – or, at any rate, much less important. Certainly, the Channel has always been, since its creation, a formidable barrier to conquest, even when its shores were defended by ill-armed and badly organized tribal systems. What pre-Roman Continental power had the resources and skills to mount a sea-borne invasion and carry through an opposed landing? The Romans themselves regarded the Channel as the final military problem. The reconnaissance in force which

St Mary's Saxon church and the Roman Pharos. 'The Romans left quite a mark on the Channel. On the cliffs east of Dover they built a remarkable lighthouse which still stands.'

Caesar landed in 55 BC created a sensation in Rome, and he was accorded an unprecedented triumph by the Senate. But both his invasions indicate the complexities of the problem. On the first occasion he got ashore eight thousand infantry in eighty transports; the cavalry never succeeded in landing at all, and the transports were nearly destroyed by storm. In 54 BC he shipped over five entire legions and two thousand cavalry, plus ballistic engines and heavy baggage, in a total of six hundred flat-bottomed ships. Even so, he was obliged to abandon any idea of permanent conquest. His landing place, somewhere near Pevensey Bay, gave no protection to his ships, which were again battered by bad weather, and he prudently gave up the expedition as a bad risk. His commentaries treat the incident laconically, but it is significant that, this time, there was no Roman triumph. Indeed, for nearly a century the Romans regarded an assault on Britain as unjustified on military and economic grounds, and it was touch and go whether they made the venture at all. The Claudian invasion was preceded by detailed planning, above all by a coastal survey which established the existence of a safe natural harbour at Richborough; and it was carried out in enormous strength, with a three-prong landing. The Romans paid the Channel the tribute of treating it with considerable respect.

The Romans left quite a mark on the Channel. On the cliffs east of Dover, they built a remarkable lighthouse which still stands, and they established three good harbours on this section of the coast, each with a government squadron of fast naval galleys for regular communication with the Continent. In the later stages of their occupation, when pirate raids from north-east Europe, beyond the Roman frontiers, became more frequent,

HIC EXE

they set up an elaborate system of coastal defences. There were at least ten sea-forts: four north of the Thames, six in Sussex, Kent and Hampshire, and probably another at Carisbrooke in the Isle of Wight. The forts, on the water's edge, had protected harbours for galleys and housed cavalry forces; the galleys acted as a deterrent, but if raiders slipped through the screen and landed, the cavalry were sent out in hot pursuit, while the galleys stood out to sea to cut off the retreat. The remnants of these fortresses survived well into Medieval times, with later castles built within their perimeter walls, as at Pevensey and Porchester. But such a system required expensive maintenance and a strong government machine. When the Roman Empire collapsed, the British colony was unable to keep the sea-defences in being; Jutes and Saxons landed in force, and penetrated inland, soon setting up independent kingdoms. The Britons never seem to have succeeded in operating regular naval forces. Nor was the Anglo-Saxon state which emerged adept at maritime warfare. It was geared to the exploitation of the land, and though it could offer formidable resistance to Danish and Viking invaders onshore, it lacked the naval organization to beat them at sea, or to launch counter-attacks on their own territory. Kings like Alfred built ships through a system of taxation and maritime service in the coastal counties; on one occasion at least Ethelred

The Norman invasion fleet nears England – an illustration from the Bayeux Tapestry. It was William the Conqueror's good fortune that the English were not equipped to challenge him at sea.

Γ:CABALI

collected a fleet, which he based at Sandwich. What the Saxons could not do, however, was to establish sea-supremacy, even for limited periods, and thus exploit the full value of the natural Channel defences.

This proved fatal in 1066. William of Normandy risked the complete destruction of his army if he was caught at sea even by modest forces. He had something like ten thousand men and four thousand horses crammed into hundreds of small ships, forty feet long with a four-foot draught, equipped with a mast and sail but no oars, and loaded, too, with a good deal of heavy baggage. This was a vulnerable target indeed, but he crossed without opposition and was able to land, as he planned, near Hastings. This was then a peninsula: he chose it as a defensible bridgehead, as the prelude to a long campaign. Before King Harold's forces arrived, after their campaign in the north, William was able to throw up an earth-and-timber fort, bring in fresh supplies, allow his men and horses to rest after their crossing, and prepare for battle. His invasion succeeded because his opponents failed to use the Channel at all; and he was doubly lucky in that, at the first engagement, Harold and his two brothers were killed, thus leaving a political vacuum which he filled without difficulty.

The Norman and Angevin kings, controlling the coasts on both sides of the Channel, had no overriding incentive to create a navy; but they were systematic men, and built on the rudimentary Saxon arrangement which obliged certain Channel ports, in return for commercial and tax privileges, to supply the Crown with ships for defence and other purposes. Even as early as Domesday Book, it is recorded that Dover undertook to convey a King's messenger across the Channel, for 2d in summer and 4d in winter. Under Henry II, in the 1170s, five of these towns, Dover, Sandwich, Romney, Hastings and Hythe, were confederated as the Cinque Ports, and granted charters which exempted them from feudal dues and port tolls, and which gave them their own courts and local government, on condition they supplied a specific number of ships for royal service. Soon, Rye and Winchelsea, classified as 'Ancient Towns', were added to the five, as were 32 lesser harbours, known as 'limbs'. The arrangement became vastly more important in the early thirteenth century, when King John lost Normandy, and with it effective control of the Channel. In 1206 he issued six new charters, one to each of the original five, and a joint one to the 'Ancient Towns'. They agreed to provide fifty-seven ships, each manned by a crew of twenty-one. Commercial, maritime and naval laws were laid down, enforced by an annual court at Shepway, and these were codified by a great charter issued by Edward I in 1278. A senior magnate was appointed Warden of the Ports, and he usually doubled up as Constable of Dover Castle.

Even so, the English kings found they had to build their own royal ships, and these were increasingly based farther down the

Channel, at Southampton, and later at Portsmouth. Indeed, during the Middle Ages, there was a growing tendency for the axis of maritime activity to shift westwards down the Channel. With the loss of Normandy, the Kent and Sussex ports became less important, while trade with Bordeaux grew rapidly, and in the fourteenth and fifteenth centuries regular commercial contacts were established with Portugal and Spain, and with great Italian cities like Venice and Genoa. Not only were the more westerly ports better placed geographically for this high seas commerce: they had much bigger, and more stable, harbours. Farther east, the continual process of erosion, subsidence and silting downgraded once-proud ports. Ships dumped their ballast at harbour entrances before taking on cargo, and this often accelerated the natural process of decay – an early example of destructive pollution. By the early sixteenth century, Sandwich was almost choked, Hastings had been strangled by obstructions, Winchelsea was closed – despite costly royal efforts at town-planning – and Hythe and Rye could take only small ships; Romney was already two miles inland.

Indeed, by this stage, only determined and constant artificial works could keep any of these old Channel ports from oblivion. Yet they were needed not only to service the short sea-passage, but to maintain English naval supremacy. The English had early appreciated that the Channel was 'English', in the sense that the comparative absence of rocks, the availability of harbours, and the prevailing winds led Channel traffic of all nations to prefer routes close to the English shore. In about 1430, a political propagandist working for the English war-party noted this fact, in his robustly patriotic poem, *The Libelle of English Policy*. England, he argued, should exploit this geographical advantage to bring pressure to bear on Flanders, Spain and other countries; Dover and Calais should be strongly defended, to exert a stranglehold on all foreign shipping in time of war:

> The true process of English policy
> From outside cares to keep this realm in rest . . .
> Is this, to south and north, to east and west,
> Encourage trade, keep naval supremacy
> That we may be masters of the narrow sea.

It was not merely a question of keeping harbours open at all, but of enlarging them to accommodate ever-bigger ships. In the early Middle Ages, ships were clinker-built, that is their planks were nailed on top of each other. Carvel-built ships, with planks flush-nailed to rib-frames, and caulked, began to be built in the Channel in the fifteenth century. These were much more seaworthy, and could carry heavier cargoes. Up until 1200 ships were steered by stern-oar (hence the word starboard, or steerboard), and double-ended. The invention of a hinged rudder, about 1200, led to a differentiation between bow and stern, and to the raking of both; raking, in turn, allowed the length of the ship to be extended beyond the keel, determined by the natural size of the oak, and thus to bigger ships, equipped with multiple masts. The medieval cog, with its single mast and sail, and limited in size to 200 tons, gave way to two- and then three-masted ships: Flanders galleasses, driven by sail on three masts and 80 oars, up to 1,200 tons, and Genoese carracks, almost as big and driven entirely by sail.

The revolution in naval architecture ended the old system of the Channel ports supplying free-enterprise ships for naval duties. Henry v built the first Channel navy: fourteen ships of over 300 tons, twenty-four medium and small ones, based on Southampton. Henry vii shifted the centre of Channel naval operations to Portsmouth where he built a dry dock and bequeathed to his son, Henry viii, seven great vessels which could fairly be called battleships. By 1514, Henry had twenty-four of them, and a proper naval infrastructure, with shipyards and depots, working under a Navy Board. At Portsmouth he experimented with giant ships, such as his 1,500-ton *Great Harry*, which proved unseaworthy. But he established the principle that quantities of heavy guns could be mounted low-down in his ships, thus providing a fairly stable platform, and allowing them to engage at long distances – the true beginning of naval warfare. By trial and error, his naval designers found that the optimum size was around 500 tons, and it was ships of this class, built under the direction of John Hawkins of Plymouth, which defeated the Spanish Armada. Raleigh noted that, although half the size of the big Spanish, Portuguese and Italian ships, they carried as many guns, and could aim and fire broadsides much faster since they could turn about in less than half the time. They could also sail closer to the wind, a vital consideration in Channel warfare: in 1588, Drake was anxious not to leave Plymouth until the Armada was actually sighted, for the fighting qualities of ships at sea deteriorated rapidly; on the other hand, when the Armada approached with a westerly wind, he had the tricky task of manoeuvring his fleet out of harbour, and getting to windward of the Spanish. He was able to accomplish this thanks to the design of Hawkins's ships, and then to wear down the Spanish by long-range bombardment. The defeat of the Armada was not an accident, but a combination of skilled seamanship and intelligent naval planning, both essentially shaped by Channel experience. And the principles of English naval policy, based on Channel warfare in the sixteenth century, were maintained until the disappearance of the all-big-gun warship in our own times.

The English did not believe the Channel could be held by naval power alone. This was why the state never allowed Dover to be destroyed by the sea. In Roman times, it was still navigable up to the present Market Square: since then, two millennia have raised the land surface by several feet. First, the estuary divided up into two channels, with a silt bank in between. By the early fifteenth century, shingle was ruining the port. A harbour arm

Henry VIII embarks at Dover for his meeting with Francis I at the Field of the Cloth of Gold (1520). Painting by an unknown artist.

was built out to sea, to hold up the shingle to the west and form a haven to the east. In Henry VIII's time, the arm was smashed by heavy seas, so the original anchorage it formed was built over, and the arm extended. Under Elizabeth, a basin was excavated, to retain the river Dour until it was unleashed in a rush to scour the sea-channel. This basin, the Pent, still forms one of the inner docks. But the shingle continued to drift round the pier-arm, and continuous efforts were made to extend and stabilize the harbour until, in the nineteenth century, the present massive harbour walls were built: and even these great sea-defences do not remove the need for continuous dredging.

Dover was thus saved, but at a huge cost justified only by its military importance. For its east cliffs form a natural defensive

216

site which has been occupied by fortifications of one kind or another since prehistoric times. The Romans were by no means the first to build there. There was certainly a fort in Saxon times, and its garrison church – brutally 'restored' in the nineteenth century – still stands, next to the Roman lighthouse. William I built his first English motte-and-bailey castle on the spot. Henry II replaced it with a much more formidable keep, and an entirely original system of concentric curtain walls and towers. So far as we know, Dover has never been taken by assault; but the French nearly succeeded in 1216, and as a result the fortifications were enlarged, and vast underground works driven through the chalk to assist communication between outlying bastions and defeat mining-attempts. That great military architect, Edward I,

1793, a cartoon map of England showing John Bull raising a wind to scatter French invasion barges.

enlarged the castle still further, as did Edward IV. And Henry VIII who, whatever his faults, seems to have set his stamp on almost every aspect of English life, and every part of the country, made Dover the keystone of the first coordinated set of coastal defences built since Roman times. Many of his forts still exist, in whole or in part: Tilbury in the Thames, Calshot, Hurst and Yarmouth in the Solent, Pendenis at Falmouth. In Kent, he protected the safe anchorage of the Downs (and denied it to enemy ships) by three circular forts at Walmer, Deal and Sandown. The last has been virtually destroyed by the sea. Walmer remains the residence of the Lord Warden of the Cinque Ports, occupied, at times, by William Pitt the Younger, Queen Victoria, and George V. There the Duke of Wellington, worried to the last by the prospect of a French invasion, died in a room preserved exactly as he left it; and the present Warden, Sir Robert Menzies, takes up his quarters there once a year. Walmer makes an enchanting and historic house, with a well-tended formal garden. But Deal has been expertly restored as the fortress Henry VIII built: a great, echoing, stone gun-platform, brilliantly planned for all-round defence by a master-architect of the Renaissance. Henry commissioned similar platforms at Portsmouth, Dartmouth, Plymouth and Fowey, and, being a thorough man, he had a pictorial record made of them, a section of which survives. At Dover, he set up batteries and blockhouses to defend the harbour: Archcliffe Fort under the Western Heights, Black Bulwark on the pier, Moat's Bulwark below the castle cliff, and another bulwark in its ditch. On the basis of Henry's defences, huge additions were made in the eighteenth and early nineteenth centuries: a ring of batteries built around the castle at the bottom of ditches, in brick, bomb-proof galleries. At one time 231 guns were mounted, ranging in size up to 13-inch mortars (though Dover's great Renaissance cannon, 'Queen Elizabeth's Pocket Pistol', was never fired in anger). On the Western Heights an entrenched and fortified camp was established to repel Napoleon's troops, if they succeeded in landing; and the thirteenth-century underground works were extended until they honeycombed the cliffs on all sides. In 1860, the Royal Commission on the Defence of the United Kingdom classified Dover as Britain's only strategical fortress, and it remained an important base in two world wars. There is nothing else quite like it in Britain – even the Tower of London. The castle and its surrounds show traces of military architecture over 2,000 years, muddled and superimposed on each other in

Below A reconstruction by Alan Sorrel of Deal Castle, one of the fortresses built by Henry VIII to guard the coasts.

Above left The first Eddystone Lighthouse, built by Winstanley in 1698 but destroyed in a storm five years later. *Right* The present, and fourth, Eddystone Lighthouse built by Sir James Douglass and illustrated here at its formal opening in 1882.

seemingly hopeless confusion and often breathtaking ugliness, yet constituting as a whole a grand and massive testimony to the strategic vitality of the Channel, and the port which commands it. Its stones almost smell of the bored sentries who have paced them over so many generations: Roman legionaries, Saxon housecarls, Angevin men-at-arms and Plantagenet longbowmen, Elizabethan cuirassiers, Cromwellian Ironsides, Hanoverian Redcoats, Marines and Tommies, Paratroopers and Commandos – a military procession stretching to the crack of doom.

Yet the Channel is infinitely more than its military and naval history. In its waters the first international rules of navigation and maritime courtesy were established, as was the unit of measurement for merchantmen, based on a tun of Bordeaux wine (252 gallons). It was Henry VIII, again, who first established the Thames pilot fraternity on a permanent basis, as the Guild of the Holy Trinity of Deptford Strond, and Trinity House still controls the key aspects of the Channel passage. Trinity House built the first Channel lights, at the North and South Foreland, in 1637; and sixty years later it set up the Eddystone Lighthouse off Plymouth. This was destroyed by the great storm of 1703, which also nearly eclipsed Brighton, and it was followed by three others, built on the same spot. Portland Bill and the Lizard got lighthouses in the early eighteenth century, and the first lightship appeared in 1732. The Channel is a complex place; its tides and shifting contours have puzzled navigators throughout its history. Its waters can only be rendered safe by an elaborate series of mechanical devices and precautions, for not only is the coast intrinsically difficult, but the high seas traffic cuts directly across the cross-Channel lanes. Sea-discipline is now more important than ever before, since 250,000-ton tankers require ten miles to come to a halt, and carry cargoes which can devastate an entire coastline.

Much of the apparatus and discipline which controls the Channel passage is invisible except to the initiated, and there are many aspects of Channel life and history which are little known. Its towns and villages are infinite in their variety. Bodiam and Camber castles were once sea-defences. Some places specialized in smuggling, which in the 1780s accounted for over twenty-five per cent of Britain's total imports. At Deal, as many as seven hundred armed men guarded the smuggling trains inland, while one thousand or more supervised the beach-landings. In January 1785, the news reached Whitehall that gales had forced the main smuggling organization to draw up its boats high on the Deal beaches (as Caesar had done eighteen centuries before), and William Pitt ordered the fleet to stand offshore while the army smashed in the boats; large-scale smuggling never recovered from this disaster. There are some curious survivals on this Channel Coast. At Buckler's Hard, Indiamen and battleships were built as late as the eighteenth century, as are yachts today. Falmouth made its living because it was a first port of call for oceanic vessels who required news from their owners about where to land their cargoes: 'Falmouth for Orders' was a regular item in sailing instructions, and 'Falmouth Quay Punts' were specially designed to carry them to ships. The port also sent out tailor's cutters, so that Atlantic passengers need not land in sea-stained clothes; and it had a brief moment of glory when it became the head-quarters for the laying of oceanic cables. The railways changed the prosperity and roles of different Channel ports just as changes in the coastline had always done. The line reached Southampton in 1840, Folkestone in 1843, Portsmouth in 1847, Plymouth in 1849 – but not until Brunel flung his majestic viaduct across the Tamar in 1859 did it penetrate into Cornwall. The railways boosted the traffic from the ocean-ports, especially Southampton, and from the few cross-Channel ports which, like Dover and Folkestone, had managed to survive. They also created entirely new centres, such as Torquay and Bournemouth. In 1841, the latter had less than thirty houses; but its pine-woods were alleged to provide 'balsamic effluvia' to cure tuberculosis, and in a generation, thanks to rail access, it was a major resort and, already, a stronghold of conservative orthodoxy.

As for crossing the Channel, it has always been a theatre for experiment. The *White Ship*, which drowned Henry I's heir, and half the nobility of Norman England early in the twelfth century, was the *Titanic* of her day. The first long-distance balloon voyage was made on 7 January 1785, when J. P. Blanchard, a Frenchman, and an American, Dr Jeffries, crossed from Dover to Calais, 'in

'The hovercraft is the present monarch of the Channel.' But for how long?

circumstances of almost unparalleled danger'. Paddle-steamers were first brought into scheduled service on this route, and Bleriot's pioneer crossing in a fixed-wing aircraft led to the first inter-state air-service across the sea. The hovercraft is the current monarch of the Channel, but men have dreamed of digging a route beneath it since at least the mid-eighteenth century, and it has been theoretically possible since the 1850s. The go-ahead for the Channel Tunnel has at last been given, and when it is opened it will bring the biggest change in cross-Channel transport since, one might say, the sea first breached those crumbling chalk cliffs eight thousand years ago. Men have hurled shells and rockets across the Channel, rowed across it and swum across it by hundreds: there is an endless fascination in the challenge of those brief twenty miles of rough water dividing a great island state from the world's largest land-mass. It is not likely to be left alone so long as humanity has the itch to devise new means of travel and propulsion.

FURTHER READING

Much of the information contained in these essays is derived from the *Victorian County Histories*, the *Dictionary of National Biography* and its various supplements, and the volumes in *The Buildings of England*, edited by Sir Nicholas Pevsner. Other works consulted include: the *Shell Guides* to England, Scotland and Wales; the Ordnance Survey maps of *Southern Britain in the Iron Ages, Roman Britain, Britain in the Dark Ages*, and *Monastic Britain*, parts 1 and 2; *English Historical Documents* (General Editor David C. Douglas); and the *Oxford History of England* (General Editor Sir G. N. Clark). More detailed studies include: Douglas Guthrie, *History of Medicine* (revised edition, London 1958); Brian Abel-Smith, *History of the Nursing Profession* (London 1960); Christopher Hill, *Intellectual Origins of the English Revolution* (1972 edition); Michael Lewis, *A Social History of the Navy, 1793–1815* (London 1960); *Thomas Creevey's Papers* (edited by John Gore, London 1949); Olive and Nigel Hamilton, *Royal Greenwich* (London 1968); Clifford Musgrave, *Life in Brighton* (London 1970); R. Manning-Sanders, *Seaside England* (London 1951); *The Diary of Francis Kilvert* (edited by William Plomer); Myles Dillon and Nora Chadwick, *The Celtic Realms* (London 1972); R. M. Lockley, *Pembrokeshire* (London 1961); J. D. Mackie, *A History of Scotland* (London 1970); John Prebble, *Glencoe* (London 1966); T. C. Smout, *A History of the Scottish People, 1560–1830* (London 1969); J. A. Williamson, *The English Channel* (London 1955); S. P. H. Statham, *The History of the Castle, Port and Town of Dover* (London 1899); L. Pearce Williams, *Michael Faraday* (London 1965); A. L. Rowse, *The England of Elizabeth* (London 1955); H. P. R. Finberg (editor), *Gloucestershire Studies* (Leicester 1957); John Smythe, *Lives of the Berkeleys* (Gloucester 1883–5); I. H. Jeayes, *A Descriptive Catalogue of the Charters and Muniments at Berkeley Castle* (Bristol 1892); Lord Campbell, *Lives of the Lord Chancellors* and *Lives of the Lord Chief Justices*; Lawrence Stone, *Family and Fortune: Studies in Aristocratic Finance in the Sixteenth and Seventeenth Centuries* (Oxford 1973); Blake Erlich, *London on the Thames* (London 1968); Michael Brander, *Over the Lowlands* (London 1965); R. W. Chapman (editor), *Johnson and Boswell: Journey to the Western Islands and A Tour to the Hebrides* (Oxford, 1965 edition); Laurence Binyon, *John Crome and John Sell Cotman* (London 1897); R. W. Ketton-Cremer, *A Norfolk Gallery* (London 1948); Martin Hardie, *Water-Colour Painting in England: Volume II: The Romantic Period* (London 1969); E. K. Chambers, *The Elizabethan Stage* (Oxford, 4 volumes, 1923); K. B. McFarlane, *The Nobility of Later Medieval England* (Oxford 1973); J. H. Plumb, *In the Light of History* (London 1972); Sidney Toy, *The Castles of Great Britain* (London, 1954 edition).

ACKNOWLEDGEMENTS

Thames Television and Weidenfeld and Nicolson would like to thank the following for their kind permission to reproduce the photographs in this book:

By gracious permission of HM the Queen, 216.
Aerofilms Limited 95 (top); Ardea Photographics 166; Brighton Corporation 193; British Museum 63, 65, 73 (bottom); British Tourist Authority 17, 22, 23, 24, 32, 60, 118, 129, 131, 160, 222; J. Allan Cash 10–11, 13, 20, 95 (bottom), 112, 130, 135, 136, 159, 204 (bottom); Colour Library International 29; A. C. Cooper 108, 216–17; Daily Telegraph 114, 124, 126; William Gordon Davis 98; Department of the Environment, Crown Copyright 2, 70–1, 73 (top), 78, 94, 103, 146–7, 152, 207, 211, 219; Mary Evans Picture Library 14, 26, 31 (right), 40, 84, 96 (bottom), 172; John Freeman Limited 38 (top and bottom), 39 (top and bottom), 58, 62, 64, 110, 218; Ironbridge Gorge Museum 170, 171; Behram Kapadia 208; Michael Holford Library 119, 132, 141, 144 (top), 196–7, 212; Keystone Press Agency 158; Mansell Collection 18–19, 19, 42, 43, 56, 74, 88, 89, 90, 91 (top and bottom), 122, 125, 138, 182, 220 (right); Mr and Mrs Paul Mellon 165; National Gallery of Scotland 52; National Library of Scotland 55; National Maritime Museum 148, 151; National Portrait Gallery 77, 104, 109, 142 (left and right), 176; National Portrait Gallery, Scotland 66–7; Andrew Paton 44, 48–9; Picturepoint Limited 47; Radio Times Hulton Picture Library 179, 185, 200, 204 (top); Ronan Picture Library 86, 96 (top), 120; Royal College of Surgeons 80, 82–3; His Grace the Duke of Roxburgh 66–7; The Royal Institution 144 (bottom), 174, 177 (top and bottom), 180, 181; Scottish Tourist Board 57; Tate Gallery 194–5, 206; Victoria and Albert Museum 203; Woodmansterne 148. Jacket illustration: the National Maritime Museum, London and Ganymed Press London Ltd.